A Capital Problem

The Attic Order and the Greek
Revival in America

A Capital Problem

The Attic Order and the Greek Revival in America

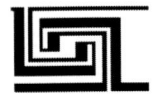

Arthur S. Marks

American Philosophical Society
Philadelphia • 2013

> Transactions of the
> American Philosophical Society
> Held at Philadelphia
> For Promoting Useful Knowledge
> Volume 103, Part 5

All rights reserved.

ISBN-13: 978-1-60618-035-8

US ISSN: 0065-9746

Library of Congress Cataloging-in-Publication Data (to come)

Marks, Arthur S., 1939-
  A capital problem : the Attic order and the Greek revival in America / Arthur S. Marks. pages
    cm. — (Transactions of the American Philosophical Society Held at Philadelphia for Promoting Useful Knowledge ; Volume 103, Part 5)
  Includes bibliographical references and index.
  ISBN 978-1-60618-035-8 (alk. paper)
  1. Architecture—Orders. 2. Greek revival (Architecture)—United States. I. Title.
NA2815.M37 2013
721'.36—dc23
                    2014025353

Contents

Acknowledgments   *vii*

1   An Ancient Order for American Architecture   1

2   Rediscovering Greek Architecture and Discovering the Attic Order   5

3   The Attic Order and English Neoclassical Architecture   15

4   The Attic Order Comes to America   33

5   Latrobe and a Capital for the Capitol   43

6   Latrobe and the Attic Order Outside Washington   53

7   Latrobe Returns to the Capitol   63

8   William Nichols and Robert Mills: Taling the Attic Order South   71

9   Taking the Attic Order Beyond Washington   81

10   American Variants on the Attic Order   97

11   The Attic Order, Its Variants, and American Domestic Architecture   113

12   The Attic Order in Decline   117

13   Yet the Attic Order Persists   127

Index   *135*

Acknowledgments

The author wishes to acknowledge a 2004 fellowship from the United States Capitol Historical Society, which aided in the preparation of this study.

1

An Ancient Order for American Architecture

— A Capital Problem —

In 1838, James Fenimore Cooper, in his novel *Home as Found*, wrote acerbically about the contemporary situation in American architecture. Speaking to Eva Effingham, recently returned to New York from an extended stay abroad, he has Aristabulus Bragg, the family lawyer, comment on the current taste in building: "I think you are mistaken, Miss Effingham, for the public sentiment just now runs almost exclusively and popularly into the Grecian School. We build little besides temples for our churches, our banks, our taverns, our court-houses and our dwellings. A friend of mine has just built a brewery on the model of the Temple of the Winds."[1] In reality, just as Bragg fictively observed, at that time a taste for the Greek was becoming increasingly dominant in the nation's architecture, though his brewery reference was no doubt intended to be facetious. Certainly no brewery appears to have been built in this manner; nor, other than for a specific detail, a capital, does this Athenian example, this Temple, or, as it is more commonly known, this Tower of the Winds, appear to have had any significant influence on the nation's architecture. But that detail (Figure 1), a capital from the Tower dubbed the "Attic order" by Benjamin Henry Latrobe, its earliest and most prominent and ardent champion, did have an enduring impact, being applied initially during the Greek Revival and persisting as a design detail well into the present. It is the history, application, and accrued meanings of the Attic order in America, together with Latrobe's role in its introduction and dispersal, that are the concern of this essay. What he saw in the Attic was a singular exception, a unique design feature, which besides having a direct and indisputable association with ancient Greece, also offered the Americans, because of the recentness of its discovery and consequently its rare application, an architectural order that might be naturalized, that might be made their own.

---

[1] James Fenimore Cooper, *Home as Found* (Philadelphia, Lea & Blanchard: 1838), 22; see also 167 for a reference to the fearful possibility of a garden folly taking the form of the Tower.

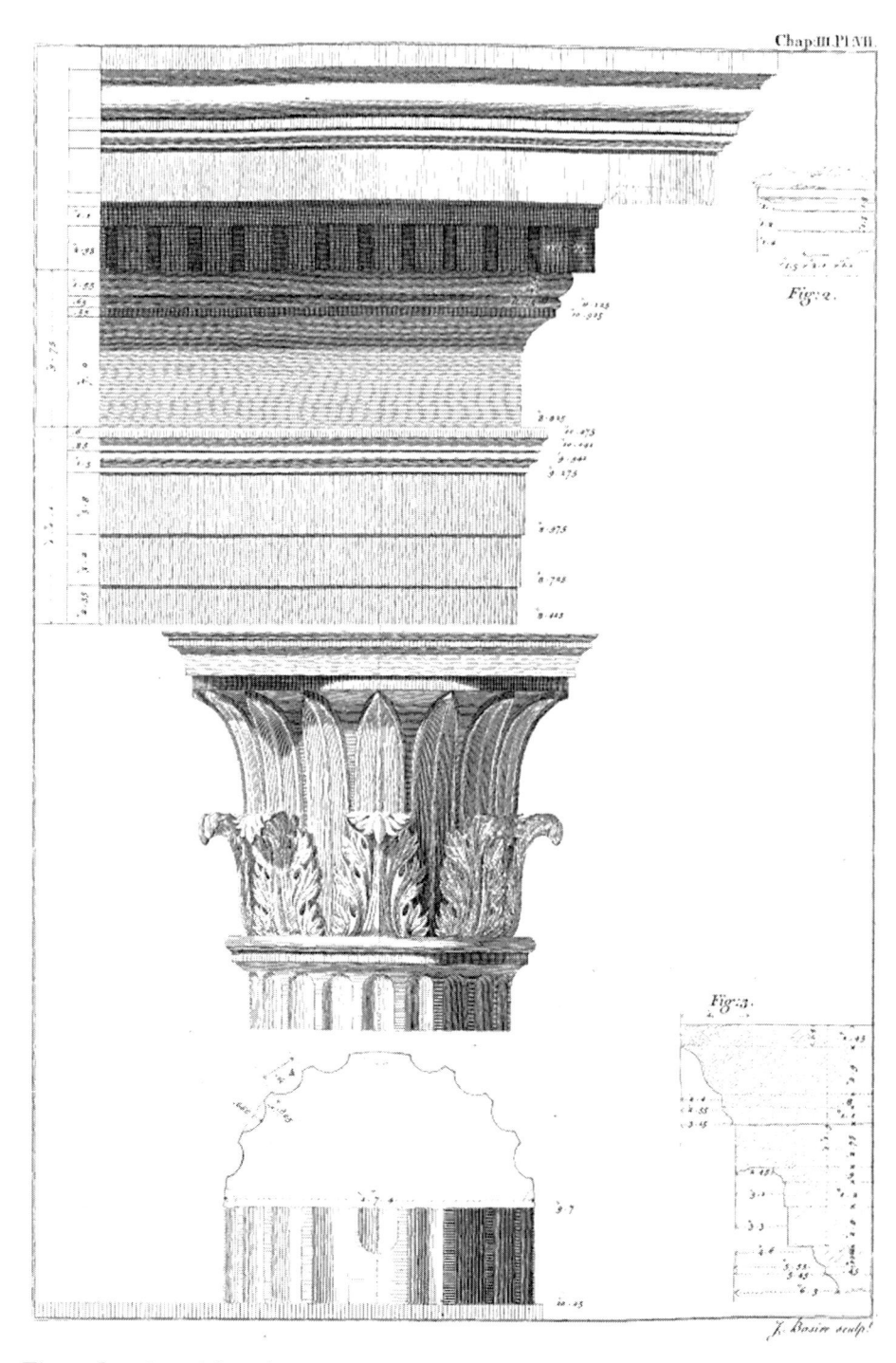

Figure 1. Capital from the *Tower of the Winds*. Engraved by James Basire.

From James Stuart and Nicholas Revett, *The Antiquities of Athens*, vol. 1 (London: J. Haberkorn, 1766), chapter 3, pl. 7.

2

Rediscovering Greek Architecture and Discovering the Attic Order

— A Capital Problem —

In his taste, Benjamin Henry Latrobe was, as he declared, a committed though pragmatic Grecian.[2] For him the perception of antiquity and the architectural models that ancient Greece offered differed sharply from the Roman past that dominated most European and American architectural practices well into the nineteenth century. Knowledge of the orders, the crucial ornamental systems that characterized ancient building styles, depended on a body of largely repetitive architectural treatises originating in the Renaissance, which went through various editions, translations, adaptations, and imitations in the succeeding centuries. Occasionally, especially during the later eighteenth century, they were refreshed by the results of archaeological investigations at Latin sites. Latrobe, however, had an entirely different perspective. He had little patience for such derivative writings and even denied their presumed authority. As he informed the diplomat and writer Joel Barlow in 1810, on whose Washington house, Kalorama, he had recently completed some work, "The books *lie*. They tell you what Palladio and Scamozzi and Vignola *opined*, not what the Greeks or Romans actually *did*."[3] With regard to the architecture of the former land he was to find one exception to this mendacity.

Turning from the Roman, from what he and like-minded architects increasingly regarded as an imitative and hybridized style, Latrobe looked instead to Greece for his sources, though again his knowledge of this past was in actuality literary. Few knew this material first hand. The Ottoman Turks, the "Barbarians," then occupied Greece and visitors from Western Europe were not welcomed to this Islamic land; it was a difficult, inhospitable, and rarely reached destination. For their knowledge of its ancient monuments antiquarians and architects depended on the publications of the few intrepid travelers who did make the journey, most notably Nicholas Revett and James Stuart, who determined to discover Greece while training as painters in Rome. Traveling east under the sponsorship of the London Society of Dilettanti, the pair was in Greece between 1751 and 1753, mainly in Athens. Most of their time was spent delineating the ruinous appearance of ancient monuments and taking carefully measured drawings of what remained. From this evidence they also

---

[2] These attitudes emerge in both his famous declaration of taste in a letter, BHL to Thomas Jefferson, May 29, 1806; John C. Van Horne and Lee W. Formwalt, eds., *The Correspondence and Miscellaneous Papers of Benjamin Henry Latrobe* (New Haven, CT: Maryland Historical Society by Yale University Press: 1984–1988), 2, 428–29; and in remarks to his building superintendent, John Lenthall, August 5, 1804, for which see *Correspondence of Latrobe*, 1 527. For the sort of statement that might have led to his pragmatism see Isaac Ware, *A Complete Body of Architecture* (London: Printed for J. Rivington, L. Davis and C. Reymers, R. Baldwin, W. Owen, H. Woodfall, W. Strahan, and B. Collins, 1768), 693.

[3] Latrobe to Joel Barlow [June 1810], Van Horne and Formwalt, *Correspondence of Latrobe*, 2, 873–74. One is reminded here of Latrobe's comment to John Lenthall, when discussing the President's house, that he felt cramped by Jefferson's "prejudices in favor of the architecture of the old French books, out of which he fishes everything": BHL to Lenthall, May 3, 1805, *Correspondence of Latrobe*, 2, 197 note 1, not a surprising taste recalling, for example, Jefferson's tuition in architecture under Clérriseau.

reconstructed what they imagined to be the original appearances of several buildings. Eventually, the studies resulting from their expedition were engraved and, with an accompanying commentary, were published in three handsome folios: *The Antiquities of Athens* appeared in 1762, 1787, 1794, with a supplementary fourth volume being issued in 1816.[4] The impact of their compendium, especially the first volume, on contemporary architecture was remarkable. Their providing apparently authentic, uncorrupted, and measured Greek models for imitation was central to the development of what William Chambers disparagingly referred to as the *Gusto Greco*, a taste that asserted the primacy of the Greek Arts over the Roman, the latter nation having "borrowed her Arts," according to Stuart and Revett, from the former.[5]

In their first volume Stuart and Revett introduced what until then was an entirely unknown ornamental order. The established Greek orders, the Doric, Ionic, and Corinthian, the canonical three, were first identified and characterized by the first-century BCE writer Vitruvius in his *de Architectura*. However, it was in their Roman versions that they had come to be depicted and deployed. To this threesome two Italian orders were eventually added, the Tuscan and the Composite, and commonly all five were illustrated for possible use by architects. With the publication of the *Antiquities of Athens*, it became possible for classical enthusiasts to discard what ultimately were derivative orders in favor of their carefully rendered authentic Greek originals. Besides jettisoning what had effectively become the five Roman columns in favor of the three Greek versions, Stuart and Revett also succeeded in expanding the canon by

---

[4] James Stuart and Nicholas Revett, *The Antiquities of Athens* (London: J. Haberkorn, 1762–94). For Stuart and Revett and the *Antiquities of Athens*, see Lesley Lawrence, "Stuart and Revett: Their Literary and Architectural Careers," *Journal of the Warburg and Courtauld Institutes* 2 (1938): 128–37; Dora Wiebenson, *Sources of Greek Revival*, 1–18; David Watkin, *Athenian Stuart, Pioneer of the Greek Revival* (London: A. Zwemmer, 1982), 15–22; Eileen Harris, *British Architectural Books and Writers, 1556–1785* (Cambridge: Cambridge University Press, 1990), 439–50; and David Watkin, "Stuart and Revett: The Myth of Greece and its Aftermath," in *James "Athenian" Stuart 1713–1788: The Rediscovery of Antiquity*, ed. Susan Weber Soros (New Haven, CT: Yale University Press, 2007), 15–57.

[5] For Chamber's remark see the third edition of his *A Treatise on the Decorative Part of Civil Architecture* (London, Printed by Joseph Smeeton, in St. Martin's Lane, Charing Cross, 1791), 26, and more extensively for his opinion on Greek architecture, which entirely omits mention of the Attic order, pp. 17–26, 38. For more on this volume and Chambers's opinions, see Eileen Harris, "The Treatise on Civil Architecture," in John Harris, *Sir William Chambers, Knight of the Polar Star* (University Park, PA: Pennsylvania State University Press,1970), 139–41; and Robin Middleton, "Chambers, W. 'A Treatise on Civil Architecture' London 1759," in *Sir William Chambers, Architect to George III*, eds. John Harris and Michael Snodin (New Haven, CT: Yale University Press, 1976), 68–76. A defensive response to Chambers appeared in the third volume, 1794, of the *Antiquities of Athens*, pp. x–xviii, and was very likely written by the editor, Willey Reveley, a former student of Chambers, whose taste had changed following a tour of Greece. Generally, on Greek versus Roman arguments, see Wiebenson, *Sources of Greek Revival*, 47–61; Eileen Harris, *Architectural Books*, 128–43; and more extensively, Damie Stillman, *English Neo-classical Architecture* (London: A. Zwemmer, 1988), 1, especially 79–136.

making a significant addition to the latter group, Latrobe's so-called Attic order, its name derived from the location of its discovery, Attica, the region of Greece that included the city of Athens.

Several times they illustrated buildings that Vitruvius had described and commented on in *de Architectura*, but whose appearances were unknown other than in implausible imaginings. Included was what the architect William Newton referred to as an "octagonal tower of marble," in another literary landmark of the Greek Revival, his 1771 translation of Vitruvius, the first in English.[6] Vitruvius mentioned this tower (Book I, chapter VI), the Horologium of Andronikos, built for the astronomer Andronicus Cyrrhestes, when discussing the passage of air currents through a walled city and the value of detecting the directions from whence the winds came. An earlier attempt at representing the building is known, but this is entirely the product of fantasy.[7] Nor is the Attic order found on the views of the tower included in other early accounts of Grecian monuments, notably two that appeared just prior to the *Antiquities of Athens*, Richard Dalton's *Antiquities in Sicily, Greece, Asia Minor and Egypt* (London, 1751–52), and the more substantial folio, Julien-David Le Roy's *Les ruines des plus beaux monuments de la Grèce* (Paris, 1758).[8] Dalton, who was well aware of Stuart and Revett's scholarly intentions, had purposefully rushed to publish first.[9] The result of a quick visit to Athens, his compendium reveals no serious archeological interest in the sites. He portrayed The Tower in its then ruinous state and offered no vision of how it originally appeared. By contrast LeRoy, from whose book Latrobe extensively copied when a student, besides showing the *Tour des Vents* embedded into its local site, also included a pair of carefully measured plans, an elevation and a

---

[6] Vitruvius Pollio, *The Architecture*, trans. William Newton (London: Printed by William Griffin, and John Clark, and published by J. Dodsley, 1771), 16–17. For the book, see Harris, *Architectural Books*,. 464–66.

[7] Titled the *Palladia Atheniesium Turris Marmorea Octogona Andronici Cyrrestis Perstructa CCCMD*: it was included in the Cesare Cesarino edition of Vitruvius; Lucio Vitruvio Pollione, *De architectura libri dece* (Como: Gotardus de Ponte, 1521), opp. p. xxv, and for the text pp. xxiii–xxiiii. With regard to the Paris, 1527, translation of this volume (*Architecture, ou Art de bien bastir*), its fantastic nature was noted by Newton in the second edition of his Vitruvius, published as *Architecture of M. Vitruvius Pollio* (London: Printed for James Newton and sold by I. and J. Taylor, R. Faulder, P. Elmsly, and T. Sewel, 1791), 1, 16–17. Depicted as a five-tiered octagonal tower decorated with extensive figural sculpture, it would impact the work of such architects as Christopher Wren and Nicholas Hawksmoor, who in imitation invented equally fantastic structures, which, however, lacked in their designs any distinct architectural order: see Wiebenson, *Sources of Greek Revival*, 65.

[8] Another appearance was in conjunction with an undated medieval tower of St. Catherine said to be a Gothic "imitation of the Temple of the eight winds at Athens," for which, see *Gentleman's Magazine* 27 (1757): 176, and the accompanying engraving of both towers, sans porch. For this reference and still other early references to the Tower, see J. Mordaunt Crook, *The Greek Revival: Neo-Classical Attitudes in British Architecture, 1760-1870* (London: John Murray, 1995; rev. ed.), 4–5, 96–97.

[9] For more on the Dalton volume, see Harris, *Architectural Books*, 173–75.

section.[10] It was not a building he admired, as it was not "estimable par les détails de son Architecture."[11] Although LeRoy suggested the one-time presence of at least one porch, not having dug at the site he offers no indication of what order might have been used for its upright supports.

By contrast to Dalton's and even LeRoy's views, Newton had observed that with the Stuart and Revett reconstruction, "we have the satisfaction of seeing the true and accurate draught of the original."[12] Now, not only could the Tower of the Winds be seen "in its present Condition," as the explorers remarked, that is, half-buried in "Soil and Rubbish" and serving as a *Teckeh*, a Turkish chapel (Figure 2), but as a result of their investigations the complete ancient structure also could be envisioned. Following their systematic excavations and with the aid of careful measurements, the pair provided a carefully devised image of the Tower's presumed original appearance. Furthermore, their diggings not only confirmed that porches had originally enhanced the two entrances but among the "Ruins of this Building" they also discovered an unfamiliar capital. They hesitated to link it definitively with the porches' columnar support, "for the upper Part of the Shaft of these Columns are broken off, and it is not possible to be certain how they finished."[13] But the capital did match a similarly carved stone that once stood at the peak of the roof and supported the triton wind vane that Vitruvius claimed had topped off the building. Despite their uncertainties, in the end Stuart and Revett did include the capital on the porches in their reconstruction (Figure 3).

Of this new order all they otherwise remarked was that "Such capitals are frequent as well at Athens as in other Parts of Greece. Altho' we do not find, that any examples of them has been hitherto published." Of its purported ubiquity they provided no evidence, but in the conventional manner for representing such details they did provide a meticulously rendered engraving of this particular specimen, with the order carefully measured and delineated from several angles (see Figure 1, p. 4). In the accepted chronological register

---

[10] Julien-David LeRoy, *Les Ruines des Plus Beaux Monuments de la Grèce* (Paris: H.L. Guerin & L.F. Delatour, 1758); for the topographical views, pt. I, 26–27, pl. xiv, and for the elevation, pt II, pls. xxvii, xxviii. Also available was a plagiarized English version, Robert Sayer, *Ruins of Athens* (London: Robert Saver, 1759), 27–28, pls. 10, 24; for which, see Marcus Whiffen, "An English LeRoy: A Plaigarization of *Ruines* which appeared in 1759," *Architectural Record* 126 (1950): 119–20; and Wiebenson, *Sources of Greek Revival*, 39–40. For a modern translation of the 2nd edition of LeRoy, *Les Ruines* (Paris, 1770), which was originally very much meant as a response to Stuart and Revett, see *The Ruins of the Most Beautiful Monuments of Greece*, introduction by Robin Middleton, (Los Angeles: Getty Trust Publications 2004), esp. 397–401, 459–50 (nn. 16, 17). For Latrobe and LeRoy see *The Architectural Drawings of Benjamin Henry Latrobe*, eds. Jeffrey A. Cohen and Charles E. Brownell (New Haven, CT: Maryland Historical Society and the American Philosophical Society by Yale University Press, 1994), 1, 68–69; and for the *Ruines* generally and their relationship to Stuart and Revett, see Wiebenson, *Sources of Greek Revival*, 33–34, 39–40, 85-87, 97; and Harris, *Architectural Books*, 289–91.

[11] LeRoy, *Ruines*,. II, 23

[12] *Architecture of Vitruvius*, 16–17 and note.

[13] Stuart and Revett, *Antiquities of Athens*, 1, 18.

— A Capital Problem —

Figure 2. *Tower of the Winds "in its present Condition."* Engraved by Anthony Walker. From James Stuart and Nicholas Revett, *The Antiquities of Athens*, vol. 1 (London: J. Haberkorn, 1766), chapter 3, pl. 1.

of canonical orders they located the new discovery between the Ionic and the Corinthian, but other than identifying it as coming from "the Octogon Tower of Andronicus Cyrrhestes," they deferred from naming it.[14]

According to Vitruvius in an often-retold account, the three Greek orders derived their names from their places of origin and the people who purportedly created them, the Doric from Doria by the Dorians, the Ionic, Ionia and the Ionians, and the Corinthian, Corinth and the Corinthians. Thus, for Latrobe, as we know from his correspondence, it followed that because this new order was found in Athens and therefore was presumably invented by the Athenians, it was fittingly called the Attic.[15] But not everyone who viewed the *Antiquities of Athens*'s engravings was convinced of the exclusivity he eventually assigned to the capital. That the Attic was entirely unlike the Doric and Ionic in appearance was easily accepted, but because it shared vegetal motifs with the Corinthian it was regarded by some as a mere variant on this third order. The architect Stephen Riou, for example, writing in *The Grecian Orders of Architecture, Delineated and Explained from the Antiquities of Athens* (London: J. Dixwell, for the author, 1768), which despite its title was decidedly Palladian in tone, sought to deny this new order any real distinction. The capital from the Tower of the Winds obtained an incidental place among his plates and of it he dismissively remarked, "whatever variety of foliage, or of other ornaments there may be to a capital, it cannot constitute a new mode."[16] Stuart and Revett, however, did distinguish between the two. They noticed the complexity of the Corinthian with its three rows of acanthus leaves, and very significantly the volutes that gave the capital its distinctive four corners. By

---

[14] Their first chapter dealt with a Doric portico, the second focused on the small Ionic Temple on the Ilissus, and the fourth discussed the Corinthian Choragic Monument of Lysicrates, a relic more commonly known as the Lantern of Demosthenes.

[15] By this name, however, it also is easily confused with another and earlier Attic or Attick order, an order of pilasters supposedly originating in Athens that were used on a building's attic story where columns were not to be installed, but rather where a continuous wall, broken occasionally by square windows, was to be ornamented by nonfunctioning pilasters and served to conceal a roof. As Isaac Ware, writing well before Stuart and Revett's discoveries, observed about this "bastard" or "false" Attic order, in his *Complete Body of Architecture* (7–8, 244–45): "We call them an order, in compliance with the common manner of expression, but they do not deserve that name." However the double meaning did not bother Latrobe and he indiscriminately used both terms; see Charles E. Brownell, "Jefferson's Canon of the Orders, Latrobe and the Interior of the United States Capitol," part of his essay "Thomas Jefferson's Architectural Models and the Unites States Capitol," in *A Republic for the Ages, The Unites States Capitol and the Political Culture of the Early Republic*, ed. Donald R. Kennon (Charlottesville, VA: United States Capitol Historical Society by the University Press of Virginia, 1999), 357–58.

[16] Stephen Riou, *The Grecian Orders of Architecture* (London: J. Dixwell, for the author, 1768), 38–39. For the book, see Wiebenson, *Sources of Greek Revival*, 42; and Harris, *Architectural Books*, 390–93. Such views of the Attic persisted. For example, John Soane in his second lecture as Professor of Architecture at the Royal Academy, first given in 1810, noted: "In the porch of the Tower of the Winds is a faint example of the Corinthian order": quoted from David Watkin, *Sir John Soane, Enlightenment Thought and the Royal Academy Lectures* (Cambridge: Cambridge University Press, 1996), 510. Similarly, some modern writers regard it in a similar manner; for example, Wiebenson, *Sources of Greek Revival*, 66–67, refers to it as "the severe semi-Corinthian Order of the Tower of the Winds."

— A Capital Problem —

Figure 3. *Tower of the Winds* as reconstructed by James Stuart and Nicholas Revett, engraved by James Basire.

From James Stuart and Nicholas Revett, *The Antiquities of Athens*, vol. 1 (London: J. Haberkorn, 1766), chapter 3, pl. 3.

contrast, the Attic capital was emphatically rounded and bell shaped, lacked volutes and cullicules and had only two registers of leaves. Like the Corinthian there were acanthus leaves at the lower register, but the vegetation above was "smooth and resemble what our Workmen call Water Leaves."[17]

Yet, what emerges of importance in these debates is that regardless of whether it was regarded as derivative or singular, the Attic capital was unquestionably acknowledged to be genuinely Greek and otherwise unfamiliar until that time. Certainly it was unknown in Roman architecture and prior to Stuart and Revett it had never been included in any of the established theoretical or archaeological treatises on which architects since the Renaissance had relied for their motifs. Consequently, its uniqueness and nationality legitimized it as a critical element for those who were committed to asserting the primacy and authority of the Greek style, even if this was to be done through the exclusive application of Grecian details.

---

[17] Stuart and Revett, *Antiquities of Athens*, 1, 18.

3

The Attic Order and English Neoclassical Architecture

— A Capital Problem —

As a building form, the rediscovered Tower of the Winds had an impact almost immediately in Britain and continued to have an influence there well into the next century. It was closely imitated as a whole, most notably by Stuart himself who, as early as 1764, reconstructed the Tower with properly detailed porches as a garden ornament at Shugborough House in Staffordshire. He recreated it again in 1784 for a banqueting house at the Mount Stewart estate in County Down, Ireland.[18] Other architects, such as James Wyatt at the Radcliffe Observatory, Oxford, 1776–94, entirely omitted the porches and the order, but played on its astronomical reference to purpose.[19] In the nineteenth century the inclusion of the tower became more playful and, recalling the earlier fantastic inventions of Wren or Hawksmoor, it was included in the spire atop William and Henry Inwood's St. Pancras New Church, 1818–22, and 1824–26, on John Soane's Holy Trinity, both in Lon-

---

[18] For these and other uses see James Lees-Milne, "Shugborough, Staffordshire, Part 1: The Park and its Monuments," *Connoisseur* 164 (1967): 211–16; James Howley, *The Follies and Gardens of Ireland* (New Haven, CT: Yale University Press, 1993), 155–60; J. Mordaunt Crook, *The Greek Revival; Neo-Classical Attitudes in British Architecture, 1760–1870* (London: John Murray, 1995; rev. ed.), 96–97; Watkin, *Athenian Stuart*, 25–27, 61–62; Stillman, *Neo-classical Architecture*, 1, 101, 103; 2, 390, 491–42; Brian Wragg, *The Life and Work of John Carr of York* (York: Oblong, 2000), 118. 130–31; and Alexander Marr, "The Garden Buildings," in *James "Athenian" Stuart 1713–1788*, 316, 332–38. However, not everyone admired the Tower as redefined in Britain. A contemporary visitor to Shugborough thought it like an "octagonal pigeon house": Lees-Milne, "Shugborough," 215. Likewise, Horace Walpole, writing to Mary Berry, September 25, 1791, denounced it as an "ugly pigeon–house": W.S. Lewis and A. Dayle Wallace, eds., *Horace Walpole's Correspondence with Mary and Agnes Berry, Yale Edition of Horace Walpole's Correspondence* (New Haven, CT: Yale University Press, 1944), 111, 357–58; and it was roundly criticized in these terms by William Chambers in some unpublished c. 1768 condemnatory lecture notes on Greek architecture; available in Wiebenson: *Sources of Greek Revival*, 46–47, 126–31. Perhaps, all had in mind James Wyatt's 1780s Tower of the Winds pigeon house at Badger Hall, Shropshire, for which, see Derek Linstrum, *The Wyatt Family, Catalogue of he Drawings Collection of the Royal Institute of British Architects* (Farnborough, UK: Gregg, 1974), 37, pl. 31.

[19] For the Radcliffe Observatory, see Antony Dale, *James Wyatt, Architect* (Oxford: B. Blackwell, 1956; rev. ed.), 82–84.

don.[20] In the United States, despite Fenimore Cooper's facetious observation, the Tower made fewer appearances. And none of these was particularly memorable—for instance, again recalling its ancient purpose and perhaps Wyatt's at the Observatory, in 1841 James Dakin incorporated a variant, the order included, as a roof structure on the Louisiana Hose Company, a New Orleans firehouse (Figure 4), and after 1848 an attenuated version served the budding astronomers at Amherst College.[21]

In common with all the orders, when detached from its ancient source, even from its supportive pillar, the Attic capital found use as an autonomous ornamental element. It could cap shafts that were fluted like the original or unfluted, and, as will be seen, was applied to a variety of building types that were not even Grecian in design. Indeed, Stuart later addressed this possibility of detachment in an advertisement tipped into the second volume, 1787, of

---

[20] For St. Pancras church, see *Survey of London*, 24 ((London: London County Council, 1952), *Kings Cross Neighborhood, The Parish of St. Pancras*, IV, 1–4; and for Holy Trinity, Dorothy Stroud, *Sir John Soane, Architect*, 2nd ed. (London, Giles De La Mare,1996), 230–33. Henry Inwood is said to have been in Athens in 1819, a trip that was noted in a reprint of *The Antiquities of Athens* (London: Priestley and Weale 1830), 45. For other English examples, see Wiebenson, *Sources of Greek Revival*, 64–66. Also it has been suggested that St. John's Chapel, Chichester, 1812–13, which originated with James Elmes and was taken up on his illness by his student John Haviland, has a floor plan that follows the Tower, for which, see Matthew Baigell, "John Haviland in Philadelphia, 1818–1826," *Journal of the Society of Architectural Historians* 25 (1966): 199–201. After emigrating to America, together with another recent arrival, Hugh Bridport, who did the plates, Haviland published a handbook, *The Builder's Assistant* (Philadelphia, 1818–21) that showed an awareness of the Tower, but made no mention of its distinct order; 1, 243–50. Interestingly, Bridport's brother George (who arrived in America prior to 1808, well before Hugh who was there c. 1818) was a close collaborator of Latrobe's, drawing for him as well as creating various decorative schemes: see Wayne Craven, "Hugh Bridport, Philadelphia Miniaturist, Engraver, and Lithographer," *Antiques* 89 (1966): 548–52; and for George Bridport's collaboration with Latrobe, see Van Horne and Formwalt, *Correspondence of Latrobe*, 2, 520–21 n. 2; 3, 836, 876 n. 6, 1003; also Cohen and Brownell, *Drawings of Latrobe*, 2, 395, 442–43, 480. In England another who used the Attic order was C.R. Cockerell, son of S.P. Cockerell, in whose office Latrobe worked from 1787–90. The younger Cockerell was in Greece from 1810–14: for his travels and use of the order see his own publication, *The Erectheion at Athens* (London, 1827); and David Watkin, *The Life and Work of C.R. Cockerell* (London: A. Zwemmer, 1974), 5–17, 160, 224, 228. Recalling Wyatt and the Tower's Oxford use an an observatory, in 1823 he had proposed using it as the model for a "Gaze Tower," for which, see 163, 150. Finally, for the use of the Tower of the Winds as a spire ornament, there is St. George's Church, Battery Point, Hobart, Tasmania, or as it was then called Van Diemen's Land. The church, 1836–3, is by John Lee Archer, an English émigré governmental architect, but the tower was added in 1847 to the design of James Blackburn, a pardoned convict, who had trained as an architect after being transported to the colony for forgery; see Roy S. Smith on Archer, and Harley Preston on Blackburn, in *Australian Dictionary of Biography*, 1 (Melbourne: Melbourne University Press, 1966).

[21] For the Hose Company, see Arthur Scully, Jr., *James Dakin, Architect: His Career in New York and the South* (Baton Rouge, LA: Louisiana State University Press, 1973), 103–04; and for the Amherst observatory, Alan Gowans, *Styles and Types of North American Architecture* (New York: HarperCollins, 1992), 110–11. Also following this model is the Daniel S. Schrank Observatory, 1865, at Rutgers University, designed by Willard Smith, for which, see Allen B. Robbins, *History of Physics and Astronomy at Rutgers, the State University of New Jersey* (Baltimore: Gateway Press, 2001), 42–43. The Tower was also used as the model for three rooftop cupolas at the Indiana Institute for the Blind, Indianapolis, 1853, by John Elder and Francis Costigan; see Gowans, *Styles and Types*, 119.

— A Capital Problem —

Figure 4. James H. Dakin, architect; plan and elevation for Louisiana Hose Company, New Orleans, 1841.

The James Harrison Dakin Collection; Louisiana Division, New Orleans Public Library.

the *Antiquities of Athens*. Responding apparently to otherwise unidentified criticisms that the initial volume only dealt with what were regarded as lesser monuments, he noted that as the authors were

> uncertain whether we should be encouraged to proceed further with this work, we selected such Buildings for our proposed publication, as would exhibit specimens of the several kinds of Columns in use among the ancient Greeks; that, if contrary to our wishes, nothing more should be demanded of us concerning Athens, those who honour us with their Subscriptions to that volume, might find in it something interesting in the different Grecian modes of decorating Buildings.[22]

In other words, if nothing else, an architect might find their compendium useful as a convenient lexicon of Greek details. As such some saw in the plates to the *Antiquities of Athens* a means by which architecture, by turning to its original sources, could be reinvigorated and regain its lost sense of order, truth, and authority.

Other than in recreations of the Tower of the Winds as follies it did not take long for this first volume to have an impact on the more practical projects of both quotidian speculative builders and architects of distinction. Even if only hesitantly in the 1770s, the Attic capital began to make its appearance on a variety of edifices, but recalling its modest supporting presence on the Tower most usages were likewise quite restrained. For example, replicating the order's original purpose, the order was used on the decorative entries and porches installed on London townhouses as part of an effort to individualize and differentiate the otherwise uniform and anonymous façades of Georgian terrace developments.[23] Even more prestigious design proposals are known but these were for unfulfilled projects and tended to lack scale and boldness. William Newton, the translator of Vitruvius and Stuart and Revett's collaborator on volume two of the *Antiquities of Athens*, unsuccessfully proposed using the Attic for an octagonal baldachino at St. Margaret's, Battersea, a London church, 1774–75.[24] Subsequently, for the

---

[22] As quoted in Watkin, *Athenian Stuart*, 19.

[23] Examples are 2 Great George Street, Westminster, and 32 Betterton Street; for which, see respectively, *Survey of London: 10; St. Margaret, Westminster, pt. 1; St. Anne's Gate Area* (London: London County Council, 1926), 17–18; and *Survey of London: 4; St. Giles in the Fields, pt. 2* (London: London County Council, 1914), 104. For the development of the town house and issues of differentiation notably on the doorcasings during the late eighteenth century, see Rachel Stewart, *The Town House in Georgian London* (New Haven, CT: Yale University Press, 2009), 129–35, 181–86. For a later and provincial use there is their appearance before several shops on the Parade, Upper Walk, Tunbridge Wells, sometimes referred to as The Pantiles after the pantiles with which this promenade was paved until 1793 when they were replaced by Purbeck stones. As the antiquarian John Britton observed in 1832, "a covered way or piazza projects" from the various shops that line the streets, which dependent on the various owners were "of varied sizes, heights and materials," and included various orders, though Britton provides no specific identifications; John Britton, *Descriptive Sketches of Tunbridge Wells and the Claverly Estate* (London: by the author, 1832), 21, 30–31, 45–46.

[24] For St. Mary, Battersea, as the drawings show, the ground floor order was Doric, which supported an Ionic gallery, and clearly in seeking a third order, even though unstacked, he turned to the Attic with its vegetation in place of the usual Corinthian: see Lesley Lewis, "The Architects of the Chapel at Greenwich Hospital," *Art Bulletin* 29 (1947): 260–67, esp. figs. 13, 14.

rebuilding, c. 1782, of the chapel at Greenwich Hospital following a fire, Newton, again collaborating with Stuart, Surveyor to the Hospital since 1758, had wanted to support the organ gallery with the recently discovered order, but this was another proposal that came to naught.[25]

For other architects, notably the brothers Robert and James Adam, both subscribers to the first volume of the *Antiquities of Athens*, the discovery of the Attic order became a liberating device. With their eclectic decorative Roman-inspired style the true Attic was more a curiosity that allowed the brothers to expand inventively their ornamental vocabulary than it was a requisite defining detail that signified a stylistic shift toward the Greek, an architecture whose primacy and purity little impressed them. Recalling its original design they created instead their own version of the Attic, the "Composed Doric" (Figure 5), which was carefully delineated in the second volume of their *Works* as published in 1773.[26] This new order was formed by combining Stuart and Revett's Attic with two capitals found during Robert Adam's 1757 excavations of Diocletian's palace at Spalatro and published in 1764 in his account of that dig, the "Second Interior Order of the Temple of Jupiter" (Figure 6), a version of the Roman Composite order, and the "Capital and Pilaster in the Angle of the Peristylium" as found on the Temple of Aescalapius (Figure 7).[27] By removing the Ionic volutes that gave the Jupiter column its frontality, the Composed Doric obtained the roundness associated with the Attic. This also allowed the upper register of leaves to be lengthened much like the water leaves of the original, but in this new capital, like the order from the Aesculapian temple, they are devoid of any naturalistic traces and appear more like a curving abstract decorative fluting.

In the *Works* the Adam brothers illustrated a range of projects, filled as they claimed with "variety and novelty." Not only was this accomplished by their use of a remarkable series of plans that incorporated a series of diversely shaped rooms that went well beyond the usual round halls and squared chambers, but it was also accomplished by the presence of their new order or variations thereof. For such usage they provided a defensive rationale:

> Nothing was more sterile and disgustful, than to see for ever the dull repetition of Dorick, Ionick and Corinthian entablature, in their usual proportions, reigning about every apartment, where no order can come or ought to come; and yet it is astonishing to think that this has been invariably the case in the apartment of every house in Europe, that has any pretentions to magnificence.[28]

---

[25] See Watkin, *Athenian Stuart*, 52–53; and for the gallery as built, Crook, *Greek Revival*, 75 and pl. 17; and Kerry Bristol, "James Stuart, The Admiralty, and the Royal Hospital for Seamen at Greenwich, 1758–1788," in Soros, *James "Athenian" Stuart*, 370–71, 376–77.

[26] Robert and James Adam, *Works in Architecture*, 2 vols. (London: printed for the authors, 1773–78), 2 (1778), pl. III. A third volume appeared posthumously (London: Priestley and Weale, 1822).

[27] Robert Adam, *Ruins of the Palace of the Emperor Diocletian at Spalatro in Dalmatia* (London: printed for the author, 1764), pls. XXXVI and XLIX, respectively.

[28] From the introduction to Adam, *Works* 1 (1773), 1–2.

Figure 5. Robert and James Adam, *"Composed Doric Order"* for the "Eating Room," Shelburne House.

From Robert and James Adam, *Works in Architecture*, vol. 2 (London: Athlone Press, University of London, for the London City Council, 1778), no. III, pl. VI.

Figure 6. Robert Adam, *Second Interior Order of the Temple of Jupiter.*

From Robert Adam, *Ruins of the Palace of the Emperor Diocletian* (London: Athlone Press, University of London, for the London City Council, 1764), pl. XXXVI.

Figure 7. Robert Adam, *Capital and Pilaster in the Angle of the Peristylium.*

From Robert Adam, *Ruins of the Palace of the Emperor Diocletian* (London: printed for the author, 1764), pl. XLIX.

— A Capital Problem —

In order to avoid such "tiresome repetition" they proposed using or actually applied some form of their "Composite Doric" on the exteriors and interiors of a series of stately homes in both London and the countryside, a good example being Lansdowne House, 1762–68, whose first sitting room and dining room (Figure 8) were preserved following its 1929 sale and rebuilding to accommodate a road widening the following year.[29] Once established, much like the Attic order, the "Composite Doric" also was applied to a number of lesser structures, often of anonymous builder's designs, yet again to the entry porches of London townhouses.[30]

The Adams' "Composite Doric" also encouraged other architects to design still further variants on it and the Attic, a good example being William Pain's "Modern Composite Capital" (Figure 9) included in his *The Practical Builder*, an oft-reprinted manual first published in London in 1774.[31] Similar designs appeared in another of his frequently reprinted handbooks, *The Practical Carpenter*, 1788, including editions in Boston, 1796 and Philadelphia, 1797.[32] Pain's volume is known to have provided American builders and architects with Adamesque classical detailing. Although not an exact copy, a comparable order was used on the eight columns that support the round and niched vestibule (Figure 10) of the Woodlands, a Philadelphia mansion, renovated 1787–89 in

---

[29] For its varied applications, see Adam, *Works*, vol. 1 (Syon House, 1762–69) pls. I.I.1, 2; (Kenwood House, 1768) I.II.4; (Luton Hoo, 1766–70); I.III.4. Royal Society of Arts, I.IV.4; and vol. 2 (1779); (Watkin-Wynn House, 1771–74) pls. II.II, 4; (Lansdowne House, 1762–67) II.II, 6. When used on the Brentford gateway to Syon House its appearance was described as "altogether new, and has been deemed not unpleasing." Interestingly, on the few occasions during the 1760s and 70s, when it was placed on an exterior monumental order, the Composite Doric was confined to lesser façades, as on the garden side at Kenwood House and the east front at Luton Hoo. On the London town house for Watkins-Wynn, St. James Square, it was used for the "Offices towards the Back." In the 1790s the Adam brothers did apply it to the monumental columns on the east and south side façades of Fitzroy Square, for which, see Alistair Rowan, *Vaulting Ambition: The Adam Bothers, Contractors to the Metropolis in the Reign of George III* (London: Sir John Soane's Museum, 2007), 32–35, 67–68. For a notable interior use, in the dining and first drawing rooms of Lansdowne House now preserved in the Metropolitan and Philadelphia Museums, see James Parker, "Patrons of Robert Adam at the Metropolitan Museum," *Metropolitan Museum Journal* 1 (1968): 117–24; and Fiske Kimball, "Lansdowne House Redivivus," *Bulletin, Philadelphia Museum of Art* 39 (1943): 2–15. For more on the Adam brothers' use of the variant capital as a decorative element, notably at the Royal Society of Arts and their adjoining Adelphi development, see Crook, *Greek Revival*, 74; John Summerson, "The Society's House: An Architectural History," *Royal Society of Arts Journal* 102 (1953–54): 920–33, esp. 932–33; D.G.C. Allan, *The Home of the Royal Society of Arts* (London: Royal Society of Arts, 1966), 11–16, 42–43; and David King, *The Complete Works of Robert and James Adam* (Oxford: Architectural Press, 2001; rev ed.), 1, 2–7, 44–46, 76–81.

[30] For example, 36 Elder Street, a c. 1725 house with later doorcase; *Survey of London: 27; Spitalfields and Mile End New Town* (London: 1957). http://www.british-history.ac.uk/report.aspx?compid=50179/. 82–84; and 32 Soho Square, c. 1773–75; *Survey of London: 33: St. Anne, Soho* (London: 1966). http://www.british-history.ac.uk/report.aspx?compid=42839/, 115–21.

[31] William Pain, *The Practical Builder*, 1st ed. (London: printed for I. Taylor, 1774), pl. XXII; and for other variants, pl. XXIV, "The Ancient Composite or Roman Capital"; and pl. XXV, "A Modern Composite Capital and Entablature." There also was a Boston edition of the book, 1792.

[32] William Pain, *The Practical House Carpenter*, 2nd ed. (London: printed for the author, 1789, the first edition being untraced), also included, pl. 21, "The Composite entablature and cap." For the different Pain books, whose plates and pagination vary from edition to edition, see Stillman, *Neo-classical Architecture*, 1, 275–76; and Harris, *Architectural Books*, 338–46.

Figure 8. Robert and James Adam, Dining Room from *Lansdowne House*, London, 1762–67, as installed in Metropolitan Museum of Art, New York.

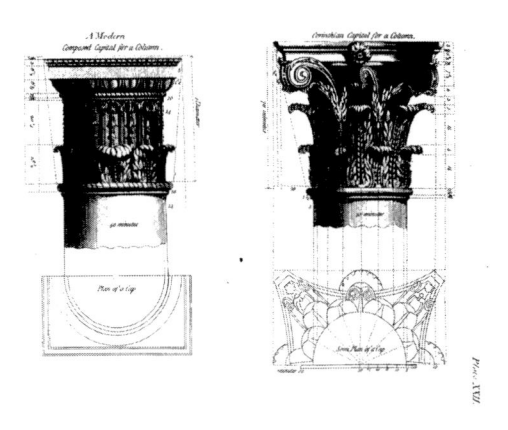

Figure 9. William Pain, *The Practical Builder* (London: I. Taylor, 1774), pl. XXII.

Figure 10. Attributed to William Hamilton the younger; vestibule, The Woodlands, Philadelphia, 1787–89.

HABS PA, 51-PHILA, 29-26.

the Adam style by William Hamilton the younger. Only recently arrived from an extended stay in England, it is thought Hamilton traveled home with plans from an otherwise unknown English architect in hand.[33] Conceivably, such decorative details as the capitals were executed by a local carpenter, who using a volume like Pain's, to whose examples it has some resemblance, added decorative features of his own.

As much as the Adam brothers and their followers found in the Attic's originality a liberating device by which a decorative liveliness could be introduced into the designing of their own ingenious orders, others saw such arbitrary transformations of the rediscovered order as leading to an eclecticism marked by stylistic corruption and decline. Although he did not specifically address issues of superiority between Greece and Rome, Sir Joshua Reynolds did take issue with such seemingly frivolous originality as the Adams' offered in his discourse delivered to the Royal Academy in December 1776. As published, he was said to have observed that:

> Though it is from prejudice we have in favour of the ancients, who have taught us architecture, that we had adopted likewise their ornaments; and though we are satisfied that neither nature nor reason are the foundation of these beauties which we imagine are in that art; yet if any one, persuaded of this truth, should therefore invent new orders of equal beauty, which we will suppose to be possible, yet they would not please; nor ought he to complain, since the old has that great advantage, of having custom and prejudice on its side. In this case, we leave what has every prejudice in its favour, to take that which will have no advantage over what we have left, but novelty, which soon destroys itself, and at any rate, is but a weak antagonist against custom.[34]

If, as Reynolds claimed, it was tradition that would prevail, then the authoritative *Antiquities of Athens* became a means by which architecture could regain its sense of order and truth. And in time in the United States, it was Benjamin Henry Latrobe who followed this advice and sought to reestablish Athens in America.

Oddly, even if only a few examples of the actual or even proposed use of the Attic order in late eighteenth-century British architecture survive or much less have been identified, that is, after its publication in 1762, there is evidence to suggest that it did actually have a more widespread usage. Unquestionably aiding in this distribution, the capital with variants appears in the 1784 catalog of

---

[33] See Sterling M. Boyd, *The Adam Style in America: 1770–1820* (New York: Garland, 1985), 185–93; and for the renovations as a whole, with no particular notice of the capitals though, see most thoroughly James A. Jacobs's addendum to the Historic American Buildings Survey, *The Woodlands*, HABS, no. PA-1125; also Jacobs, "William Hamilton and the Woodlands: A Construction of Refinement in Philadelphia," *Pennsylvania Magazine of History and Biography* 135 (2006): 181–209; now superseded by Richard J. Betts, "The Woodlands," *Winterthur Portfolio* 14 (1979): 213–34.

[34] Initially published in Joshua Reynolds, *A Discourse, Delivered to the Students of the Royal Academy on the Distribution of the Prizes, December 10, 1776* (London: Thomas Davies, 1777), 39.

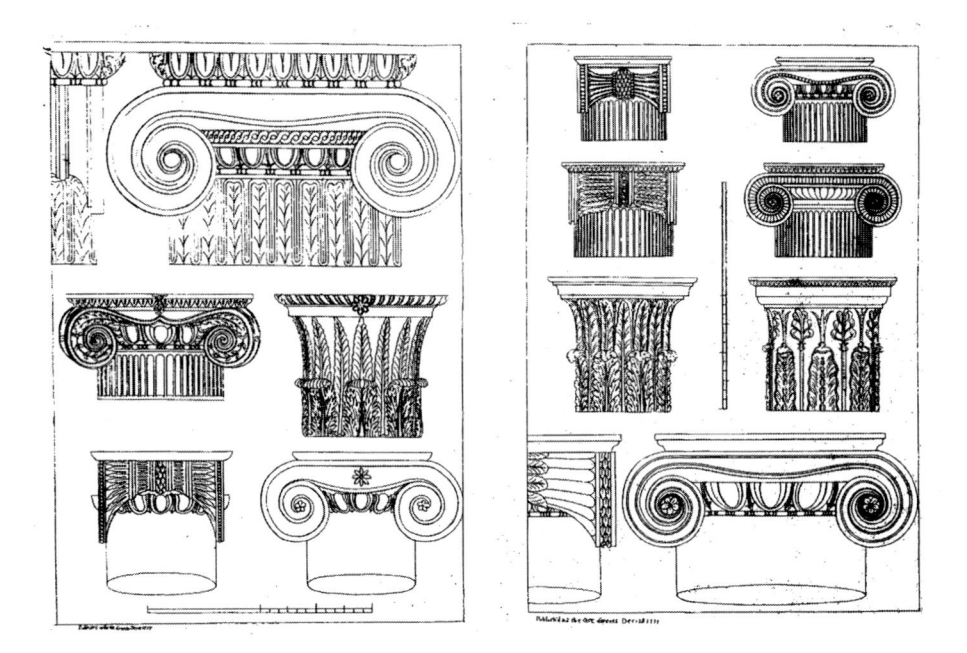

Figure 11. (a) A composed capital and (b) a fancy capital, engraved, 1777, as included in *A Descriptive Catalogue of Coade's Artistic Stone Manufactory* (London: Author, 1784).

Coade's Artistic Stone Manufactory, where it is listed as "A Composed Capital" and "A fancy Capital" (Figure 11). In fact, the first castings in this artificial stone well predate the catalog listings, as the corresponding engraved illustrations date to 1777.[35] What is particularly significant in the present instance, however, is that in an exhaustive study of the Coade works, a manufactory founded in 1769, the sole identified use of cast Attic capitals was at Ashdown House, a Sussex country house designed in 1792 by Latrobe, who had only recently started his own architectural practice. It was built between 1793 and 1794, just prior to Latrobe's departure for America.[36] Besides applying a Coade version of the Ionic derived from the second volume of the *Antiquities of Athens* to the entry porch and upstairs, on the first-floor landing, Latrobe also framed all three

---

[35] *Descriptive Catalogue of Coade's Artistic Stone Manufactory* (London: Author, 1784), nos. 165–66, 180–81.
[36] See Alison Kelly, *Mrs. Coade's Stone* (Upton-upon-Severn: Self Publishing Association 1990), 102, 151, 155–56, 379.

bedrooms with a pair of columns capped with "fancy" capitals (Figure 12).[37] The use of Coade items at Ashdown is further confirmed by the house's inclusion in a 1799 Coade catalog list of places where "our Works have been Executed."[38]

---

[37] For the house, see Jeffrey A. Cohen and Charles E. Brownell, *The Architectural Drawings of Benjamin Henry Latrobe* (New Haven, CT: 1994), 1, 53–55, where no notice is taken of the use of the Attic order, much less the use of Coade stone, but an Englishman's account of his travels in America, printed in the August 28, 1805, *Federal Gazette and Baltimore Daily Advertiser*, praises its Grecian details and remarks with reference to the English topographic artist Thomas Malton: "and the stair-case and landing place above, is a picture worthy of Malton's pencil"; from the letter as quoted in Christopher Richmond, *A History of Ashdown House* (Burgess Hill: privately printed, 1991), 6–7. Also see Michael W. Fazio and Patrick A. Snadon, *The Domestic Architecture of Benjamin Henry Latrobe* (Baltimore: Johns Hopkins University Press, 2006), 170, 172–76. Given the date of the repaving of the Parade at Tunbridge Wells noted above and the contemporary building of Ashdown fourteen miles away, the possibility remains of some connection between these two uses of the Attic.

[38] Also listed is Latrobe's use of Coade stone at Hammerwood, a nearby house he designed in 1793, though with no Attic details; *Coade's Gallery, or, Exhibition in Artificial Stone* (London: S. Tibson, 1799), x; also in Cohen and Brownell, *Drawings of Latrobe*, 1, p. 68.

Figure 12. Benjamin Henry Latrobe, Ashdown House, 1792–94, Forest Row, East Sussex, England.

Photo by the author.

4

The Attic Order Comes to America

— A Capital Problem —

By the time Latrobe arrived in America, landing in Virginia in March 1796, the works of Stuart and Revett already were well known there to architects and master carpenters, as well as being more widely available in subscription libraries or the collections of learned persons.[39] "The Library at Philadelphia; Benjamin Franklin, Esq.," that is, the Library Company, the subscription library founded by Franklin and friends in 1731, is listed among the subscribers to the initial volume, and between 1785 and 1789 Jefferson is known to have obtained the same volume while abroad. Another copy was at Harvard, and if Latrobe's own copy did not accompany him on the sea voyage, it certainly did eventually reach his hands.[40] Otherwise, at least in publications, Stuart and Revett's Attic was rarely, if ever, to be encountered. Almost incidental in its inclusion and much less detailed in presentation, it was depicted among the other Greek orders in Riou's *Grecian Order*, but other than the Coade catalog it makes no appearance in such popular guides to classical architecture as the various volumes of Pain or Peter Nicholson.[41] Rather it was the canonical three, the Ionic, Doric, and Corinthian, whether in their purer Greek form or as corrupted by the Romans, that consistently prevailed.[42] But, for the cognoscenti, those whose education and taste might encourage a distinctly Grecian architectural statement, the Attic order repeatedly came to the fore as an alternative.

This difference in approach to the order, whether using the Attic as part of an eclectic, largely Roman-flavored design like that of the Adam brothers or employing it antidotally, for its chastening qualities, is readily evident in what apparently are the Attic's earliest appearances in America, in virtually

---

[39] For its presence and impact in America, see David Watkin, "Epilogue: The Impact of Stuart over Two Centuries," in Soros, *James "Athenian" Stuart*, 534–39; and for its availability in Boston and at Harvard, Harold Kirker, *The Architecture of Charles Bulfinch* (Cambridge, MA: Harvard University Press, 1969), 4–5. For the Grecian revival in America, the standard and fullest account remains Talbot Hamlin, *Greek Revival Architecture in America* (New York: Oxford University Press, 1944), but also see Gowans, *Styles and Types*, 82–129; Roger G. Kennedy, *Greek Revival America* (New York: Stewart, Tabori & Chang, 1989); and W. Barksdale Maynard, *Architecture in the United States, 1800–1850* (New Haven, CT: Yale University Press, 2002), passim. Also see Giles Worsely, *Classical Architecture in Britain: The Heroic Age* (New Haven, CT: Yale University Press, 1995), 278–87.

[40] See Jeffrey A. Cohen, "The Architectural Libraries of Benjamin Henry Latrobe," in *American Architects and Their Books to 1848*, eds. Kenneth Hafertepe and James F. O'Gorman (Amherst, MA: University Of Massachusetts Press, 2001), 109–10; and for his use of the *Antiquities of Athens*, see Latrobe to Jefferson, November 17, 1804: *Correspondence*, 1, 571–72.

[41] The order finds no mention, for example, in William Pain, *The British Palladio* (London: H.D. Steel, 1786 and subsequent editions, 1788, 1797), or Peter Nicholson, *The Student's Instructor in Drawing and Working the Five Orders of Architecture* (London: Printed for I. and J. Taylor, at the Architectural Library, No. 56, High Holborn, 1795), nor in Peter Nicholson, *An Architectural Dictionary* (London: J. Barfield, 1811–19), though in 1, 294–95, he does mention the Tower, but the capital is included in the second edition, that is, *Encyclopedia of Architecture; being a new and improved edition of Nicholson's Dictionary of the Science and Practice of Architecture*, eds. Edward Lomax and Thomas Gunyon (London: Peter Jackson, 1852), 1, 201 and Corinthian Order, plate ii.

[42] See the extensive discussion in Hamlin, *Greek Revival in America*, 340–55.

Figure 13. Benjamin Henry Latrobe, elevation for Mill Hill House, 1796, design for an unbuilt house in Virginia.

In the collection of the Library of Congress.

simultaneous though contrasting uses by Latrobe and Charles Bulfinch. As the new nation's most avid advocate of the Greek Revival, Latrobe also proved to be its most prolific user. As it was entirely unmediated by the Romans, for him the Attic was the exception that might confirm this new style. Certainly it was a distinct marker of it. Initially, yet again he applied the Attic to a domestic project, where recalling the Athenian Tower, it is used for the supports of an entry porch. The capital appears in the designs for Mill Hill, a large Virginia house apparently never built and about which little is known beyond several drawings (Figure 13). Neither its intended patron nor its specific location has been identified and even the dating is uncertain. It might have been drawn as early as 1796, but very likely it was planned three years later.[43] Indeed, it is not unlikely that he even proposed using the order in a Coade version. Other builders and architects in America were already importing Coade components and Latrobe too would eventually resume using them.[44] Given his familiarity with their convenience as ready-made elements and their proven availability through shipping, the finished imported versions may well have had a strong appeal. Furthermore such precast capitals were a very welcome

---

[43] For a full discussion of the project and the known drawings, including its appearance on the frontispiece to Latrobe's unpublished *Designs of Buildings Erected or Proposed to be built in Virginia*, 1799, see Cohen and Brownell, *Drawings of Latrobe*, 1, 80–81 and 90–98; also Fazio and Snadon, *Domestic Architecture of Latrobe*, 227–29.

[44] For a list of early American uses, see *Coade's Gallery*, xii; which includes "WASHINGTON, New Foederal City, Capitals, Frizes, Key Stones, Chimney-pieces, & c." It also was available in Philadelphia at William Bingham's and John Dorsey's, as well as at Boston, which further suggests its use by Bulfinch and others; Kelly, *Coade*, 281–93.

resource in a land that he soon realized was deprived of stone carvers sufficiently skilled to competently execute such detailed work. But all evidence is that Mill Hill never proceeded beyond the design state.

Little noticed is Bulfinch's early usage of the order. It was first commented on by his great admirer Asher Benjamin in his practical handbook, *The American Builder's Companion* (1st ed., Boston, 1806). In this derivative text in which Benjamin sought to identify elements that might comprise an architectural style suitable to America, the Attic was included, but any mention of its archaeological origin and published source was omitted. However, for him, shown with some derived designs, plate 23, numbers 2 and 3, it was a very minor ornament and he disparagingly observed of his number 5 (Figure 14), the Attic: "This capital is not fit for every situation, but will answer for windows or shopfronts. It was used in the windows for the statehouse, in Boston by Charles Bulfinch, Esq. where it is well adapted."[45] A serious admirer of the Adam brothers, whose London work he saw during a tour abroad, 1785–87, Bulfinch's use of the Attic capital for the pilasters that frame the principal floor windows on the outside wings of the Massachusetts State House, 1795–98 (Figure 15), directly recalls the pilaster capitals at the Adelphi. Also, following that precedent, this was a distinctly Roman use of the Attic, for a proper Grecian would only place the canonical orders atop a column and never flatten them out on a pilaster.[46] Curiously, by the third edition of his *Companion* (Boston, 1816), Benjamin omitted all reference to the State House and the order was even more dismissively cited as appropriate only "where lightness is required, and when the expenses of the Corinthian is to be avoided."[47] But,

---

[45] Asher Benjamin, *The American Builder's Companion* (Boston: Etheridge and Bliss, 1806), 42 and pl. 23 no. 5. Hamlin's discussion of Benjamin, Bulfinch, and their taste for the Adam brothers in the context of American classicism remains pertinent: *Greek Revival in America*, 91–96.

[46] Conceivably, Bulfinch even used the Attic earlier, on the first Joseph Coolidge house, Boston, 1791–92, where, in a design that clearly derives from the Society of Arts and anticipating the Venetian window at the State House, he placed such a window at the center of the principal floor, but like the Adam brothers, he framed it with attached columns, possibly with Attic details rather than pilasters: see Kirker, *Bulfinch*, 41–44. Subsequently, he also used the Attic on the Venetian window of the Harrison Gray Otis House, Boston, 1795–96 (and since much restored and altered), a house whose façade depends on the William Bingham house in Philadelphia, c. 1787, which Bulfinch drew during a visit of 1789, and for which, see William and Thomas Birch, *The City of Philadelphia in the State of Pennsylvania as it appeared in 1800* (Philadelphia: W. Birch, 1800), pl. 19; Henry A. Boorse, "The Third Street House in Philadelphia by William Birch; The Inside Story," *Imprint* 14, no. 2 (1989): 11–17; and Kirker, *Bulfinch*, 119–121. To judge from Bulfinch's drawing, the Bingham house, long since razed, also may have had the Attic order on its Venetian window. Interestingly, all these projects employed Coade stone elements decoratively, and the question arises as to whether they also were used for the capitals: see the discussion in Kelly, *Coade*, 286–93.

[47] Benjamin, *American Builder's Companion*, 3rd ed. (Boston: R.P. & C. Williams, 1816), 50 and pl. 22 no. 5. It was not until the fifth edition, 1826, that he would show authentic Greek versions of the orders rather than Roman variants: see Hamlin, *Greek Revival in America*, 163–64; and Jack Quinan, "Asher Benjamin and American Architecture," *Journal of the Society of Architectural Historians* 38 (1979): 245–49, and for its application in his own practice, 249–54.

Figure 14. Asher Benjamin, *American Builder's Companion* (Boston: Etheridge and Bliss, 1806), pl. 23.

Figure 15. Charles Bulfinch, Massachusetts State House, Boston, Massachusetts, 1795–98. Photo by Terry Rosenberg.

as will be seen below, years later, after having undergone a significant change in taste, Bulfinch would return to the Attic order, applying it this time on a monumental project that very likely was conceived as a posthumous salute to Latrobe.

Although Bulfinch apparently long disregarded the Attic in succeeding years, for Latrobe it emerged as a major architectural component, which, rather than being sequestered away on private houses, was meant to be prominently displayed on public edifices. Initially, as a giant order, he included it on his unsuccessful submission to the competition held between February and April 1802 for a new city hall for New York City. Unlike the winning French-inspired design of Joseph Magnin and John M. McComb, Jr., with what he regarded as its excessive and poorly integrated volumetric massings, Latrobe offered a compact building with a clear geometry marked by a distinctly Greek-styled temple entrance (Figure 16). As several drawings for the project indicate, he rested the pediment that crowned the portico on a series of unfluted

Figure 16. Benjamin Henry Latrobe, *design of a city hall proposed to be built in New York*, 1802.

columns, all with Attic capitals.[48] Had Latrobe's plan been selected and built, it would have been an early and prominent monument to the Greek Revival in America, a celebrated public building wholly of his own design. As it was, his next proposed use of the order, although it came on a far more significant structure, the Capitol then being built in Federal City, the nation's recently designated capital, nevertheless only permitted him to offer the Attic as an added element in what was essentially an inherited design of decidedly Roman bias whose overall integrity he was under great pressure to respect.

---

[48] For Latrobe's design, see Cohen and Brownell, *Drawings of Latrobe*, 1, 303–25; and more generally for the competition, Damie Stillman, "New York City Hall: Competition and Execution," *Journal of the Society of Architectural Historians* 23, no. 3 (1964): 139–42.

5

Latrobe and a Capital for the Capitol

— A Capital Problem —

It was Thomas Jefferson, who in March 1803, appointed Latrobe Surveyor of the Public Buildings of the United States. And it was Jefferson's taste that Latrobe had to deal with when completing a structure that was well advanced in design and construction when he came to the post.[49] Initially, as Secretary of State under Washington, 1789–94, subsequently during his service as vice president under John Adams, 1791–1801, and finally as President, 1801–09, Jefferson took overall charge of the planning and construction of the United States Capitol. He is understood to have wanted the Capitol to be a didactic showcase of the architectural orders, specifically the three canonical orders, but in their Roman variants. A Roman Doric was to be displayed in the House of Representatives, an Ionic version in the Senate, and reserved for the exterior façades was the Corinthian.[50] For the exclusively Latin orders, the Tuscan and Composite, that he and many others regarded as post-antique inventions, Jefferson had little regard. Consequently they lacked any real authority for inclusion on a building that sought to simulate an ancient Roman past with its historical legacy of democracy and republicanism.

Following a competition won by William Thornton, a physician and amateur architect, work on the Capitol commenced in 1793. Nevertheless, in the immediately succeeding years there followed a series of alterations to Thornton's design from Jefferson and several architects working under his supervision, notably Stephen [Etienne] Hallett, George Hatfield, and, yet again, Thornton. Consequently, when Latrobe became Surveyor in 1803, with the confusion that resulted from so much interference, indecision reigned and only limited progress had been made in construction. He arrived at a project in which the north wing that housed the Senate was thought to be largely complete, but work on the central domed section as called for in the plans had not properly begun. Also, beyond the foundations and the beginnings of the oval hall within which the House of Representatives was to convene, little advancement had been made on the south wing. Latrobe would remain in charge of design and construction at the Capitol until 1811. He would return to the building from 1815 to 1817, when damage from the purposeful 1814 fire set by the British during the War of 1812 required extensive reconstruction.

---

[49] For the position, see Ralph E. Ehrenburg, "Mapping the Nation's Capital: The Surveyor's Office, 1791–1818," *Quarterly Journal of the Library of Congress* 36 (1979): 309–16; and an editorial note, "The Surveyorship of the Public Buildings," in Van Horne and Formwalt, *Correspondence of Latrobe*, 1257–60. And for some insights into Latrobe in this position and its tensions, see Jeffrey A. Cohen, "Forms into Architecture: Reform Ideals and the Gauntlets of the Real in Latrobe's Surveyorships at the U.S. Capitol," *The United States Capitol, Designing and Decorating a National Icon*, ed. Donald R. Kennon (Athens, OH: United States Capitol Historical Society by Ohio University Press, 2000), 23–55.

[50] See Brownell, "Jefferson's Canon of the Orders," 349–81; and for a brief discussion of Latrobe and the orders, see Cohen and Brownell, *Drawings of Latrobe*, 1, 11–15.

During his first campaign he undertook completion of the north wing as the most immediate task.[51] On the exterior, replicating the features of the south wing, the façades would again be Corinthian. As he later recalled in a letter to the Congress, "from that there could be no deviation."[52] For reshaping the interior, in the inaugural status report of April 4, 1803, which he forwarded to Jefferson, he recommended that the colonnade that surrounded and defined the House chamber be "of a freestone series of columns of the Corinthian or Attic order," that were 2'6" in diameter and stood 25 feet with a five-foot-high entablature above.[53] However, this initial attempt to introduce the Attic on such an unprecedented scale was to no avail and Latrobe was quickly forced to give way to Jefferson's taste for Doric columns, but with bases in the Roman manner. This predilection for the Doric may have had symbolic underpinnings. Unlike the Senate whose members represented the various states, the House, having been directly elected by a broad section of the expanding (male) American population, epitomized the base on which the government's authority rested. Therefore it warranted use of the Doric not only as the earliest order, but also because metaphorically it was characterized as the strongest and most masculine. Disregarding such symbolic considerations, Jefferson was taken to task by his architect, who dismissed his selection as architecturally unsuitable. Not only was Latrobe uncomfortable with a hybridized order, the Roman Doric, referred to by Riou as a "vulgar modern error," but more important, as he sought to demonstrate in a March 1804 drawing (Figure 17), he also found that the requisite frieze was entirely unsuited to such an installation. When following the colonnade's curvature, he found that the metopes had their forms distorted from the standard square to an oblong shape.[54]

Having identified the failings of the Doric order for the House's colossal colonnade, Latrobe now became more assertive. Seeking to make the chamber's interior more emphatically his own, in another drawing from the same month he again offered Jefferson the alternative of massive columns in the Attic order

---

[51] For Latrobe's first campaign, see Cohen and Brownell, *Drawings of Latrobe*, 2, 327–424; Talbot Hamlin, *Benjamin Henry Latrobe* (New York: Oxford University Press, 1955), 256–92; and more generally, William C. Allen, *History of the United States Capitol* (Washington, DC: U.S. Government Printing Office, 2001), 49–95

[52] From "A Private Letter to Members of Congress," November 28, 1806; Van Horne and Formwalt, *Correspondence of Latrobe*, 2, 306. Unsuccessfully, however, in 1811 he did suggest some Greek touches on the exterior, notably a proposal for a sculpted frieze in the manner of the Parthenon at the base of the central dome and somewhat apart from the building, to the west a Doric propylaea gateway; see Cohen and Brownell, *Drawings of Latrobe*, 2, 55–56.

[53] The report is reprinted in Van Horne and Formwalt, *Correspondence of Latrobe*, 1, 268–84.

[54] Riou, *Grecian Orders*, 25. For the accompanying letter to Jefferson in which he identifies this Doric as being "similar to Vignola's representation of the Doric of the Theatre of Marcellus," whose proportions he would use, see BHL to Jefferson, March 29, 1804: Van Horne and Formwalt, *Correspondence of Latrobe*, 470–7, and for the distortions, 466–67. For an extensive discussion of this drawing, the only surviving sheet from a packet of five that accompanied this letter, see Cohen and Brownell, *Drawings of Latrobe*, 2, 374–77.

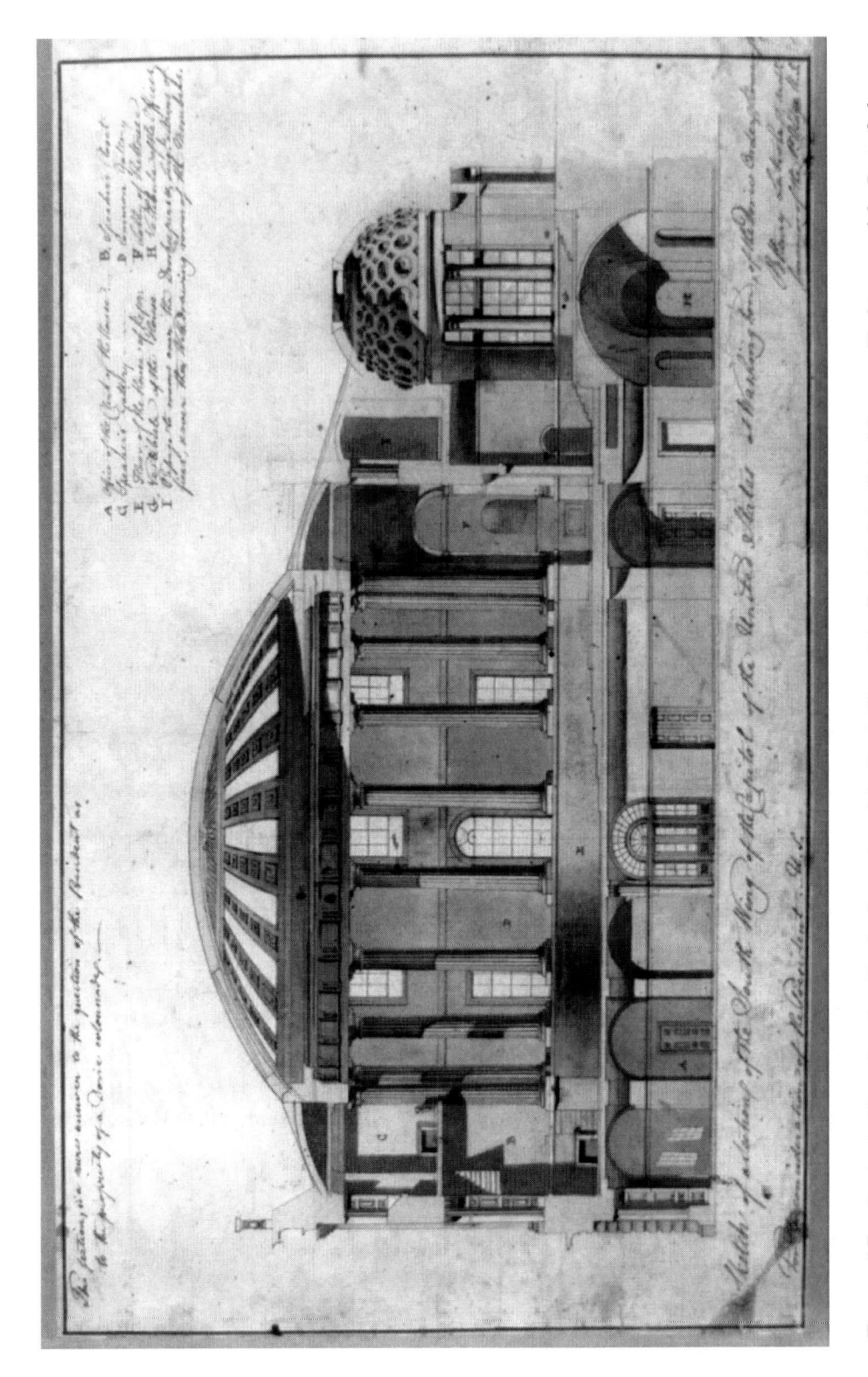

Figure 17. Benjamin Henry Latrobe, *Sketch of a section of the South Wing of the Capitol of the United States at Washington, of the Doric Order, Roman Style*, March 1804.

Library of Congress, Prints and Photographs Division.

(Figure 18).[55] Of it he remarked, "The Columns are of the Attic order, a very beautiful specimen of which is to be found in the Clepsydra at Athens, commonly called the Temple of the Winds (see Stuart's *Athens*)."[56] Finally, convinced by Latrobe's arguments about the ill proportions of the frieze, Jefferson conceded a few days later by post that "the Doric order for the Representatives' chamber must be given up," but still he was not prepared to yield and accept the obscure Attic. Instead he insisted that, "as the Senate Chamber is Ionic, we must make this Corinthian, and do the best we can for the capitals and modillions."[57] His rejection of this new order may reflect his Roman bias, but at the same time, though it did not find any place within his architectural vision, Jefferson does appear to acknowledge the Attic's validity as a distinct fourth ancient order.

Regardless of the President's decision, Latrobe continued pushing for the Attic. His reasons for doing so quickly became evident and they extend well beyond any debates about the superiority of Rome or Greece. Instead they reach into the realm of the purely practical, into issues of fabrication. Continuing in his letter to Jefferson, he noted that:

> The Doric order being given up, and the Corinthian adopted, I must consider in what manner the Capital can best be made: There would be no difficulty whatever in casting the Attic capital of the Clepsydra, because all the upper plain leaves would be cast with the bell, and the lower, raffled, leaves would be easily rivetted on, being cast either in Brass, or Iron. The capital would, thus require only 2 patterns and moulds. But the Volutes of the Corinthian Capital would require many moulds, and very nice Manipulation. . . . This I submit to your consideration. The Athenian capital I allude to, is of the best Age of Athenian architecture, as is to be found in the 1st. or 2nd. Volume of Stuart's *Athens*. The exterior decorations of the house furnish a very good specimen of Corinthian Architecture. Should you however prefer the same order for the Hall of Representatives I will immediately proceed to make the necessary drawings, and take the steps to have the Capitals executed during the present season.[58]

What Latrobe had discovered was a persistent difficulty in finding sufficient numbers of skilled stone carvers to carry out the demanding ornamental work required for the Capitol, to the point that he was forced to solicit and recruit workmen from Italy, most notably the brothers-in-law Giovanni Andrei and Giuseppe Franzoni.[59] Given the number of columns required for the House hall, even

---

[55] This sheet is an apparent replica of a lost sectional study that also formed part of the parcel sent to the Vice-President, March 29; see Cohen and Brownell, *Drawings of Latrobe*, 2, 377–80.

[56] BHL to Jefferson, March 29, 1804: Van Horne and Formwalt, *Correspondence of Latrobe*, 2, 469–70.

[57] Jefferson to BHL, April 9, 1804: Van Horne and Formwalt, *Correspondence of Latrobe*, 1, 475.

[58] BHL to Jefferson, April 29, 1804: Van Horne and Formwalt, *Correspondence of Latrobe*, 1, 485–86.

[59] See Phillip Mazzei to BHL, September 12, 1805: Van Horne and Formwalt, *Correspondence of Latrobe*, 2, 141–45; and for the difficulty of securing sufficient craftsmen, a problem that plagued him throughout his Capitol years, see Charles E. Brownell, "Latrobe, His Craftsmen, and the Corinthian Order of the Hall of Representatives," in *The Craftsman in Early America*, ed. Ian Quimby (New York: W.W. Norton, 1984), 259–60.

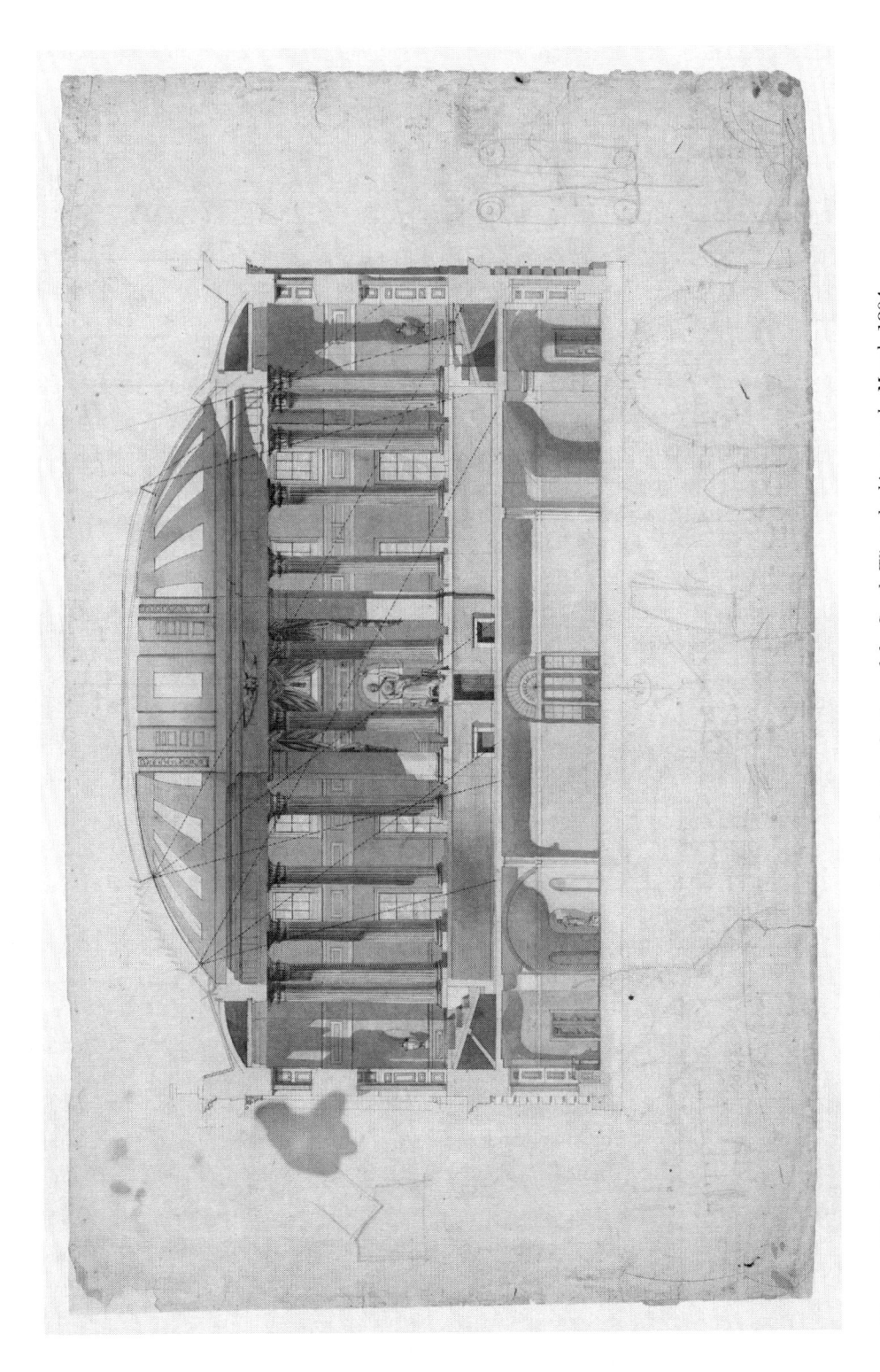

Figure 18. Benjamin Henry Latrobe, replica of a lost drawing, *Section of the South Wing, looking south*, March 1804. Library of Congress, Prints and Photographs Division.

if reduced from the thirty-two mandated by Thornton's plan to the twenty-four he recommended, the possibility of casting the capitals in iron must have been an attractive expedient and economic alternative.

Jefferson was having none of this. Disregarding Latrobe's concerns about the difficulties to be encountered in fabricating capitals, he persisted in insisting on the Corinthian. Moreover, he had a specific version in mind. He wanted the Corinthian as found in the Roman Forum on the remains of what was then identified as the Temple of Castor and Pollux, the long-admired design of which was conveniently available on a detailed plate in various editions of William Chambers' *Civil Architecture*. Giving it further credence, it also was illustrated in Palladio's *Four Books of Architecture* and other early volumes on Roman antiquities.[60] Yet even here subterfuge prevailed. Disregarding the President's choice, Latrobe introduced instead a Greek Corinthian. As he wrote John Lenthall, his trusted site superintendent, on October 29, 1804, "I have followed the Greek rather than the Roman Style, in spite of Sir William Chambers."[61] His preference was the Corinthian of the Athenian Choragic Monument, the so-called "Lantern of Demosthenes" that had been carefully documented by Stuart and Revett in the chapter immediately following their discussion of the Tower of the Winds.[62] For the accompanying cornice though, Latrobe did accede to Jefferson's wishes and, turning to Chambers, he detailed it from the Temple of Castor and Pollux.

Having lost the struggle to use the Attic order in the House itself, Latrobe nevertheless must have found some pleasure with his successful transformation of this prominent space through the monumental use of another authentic Greek element, though again it was the elevation of what was ostensibly a minor detail, the Choragic Corinthian, into a major presence. But his attempt to introduce the Attic was not entirely abandoned. What tends to go unnoticed in the sectional south-wing drawing (see Figure 17, p. 47) and the accompanying letter of March 1804, in which Latrobe demonstrated the distortions affecting the Doric frieze, is the transformation of what ostensibly had been a passageway on the principal floor between the Capitol's central rotunda, the "Hall of the People," according to Jefferson, and the House of Representatives. By his own design and as built, he successfully introduced here a domed anteroom, the "Vestibule of the House," as he labeled it, and an adjoining "Principal Stairs."

Although lesser public spaces they were his own and the prominence he sought for them is readily evident in a November 1807 descriptive letter to the editor

---

[60] Isaac Ware, *The Four Books of Andrea Palladio's Architecture* (London: Isaac Ware, 1735), 104 and pls. lxix, lxx.

[61] *Correspondence of Latrobe*, 2, 553.

[62] See Stuart and Revett, *Antiquities of Athens*, 1, 27–36; and for his use of this volume, BHL to Jefferson, Nov. 17, 1804, see Van Horne and Formwalt, *Correspondence of Latrobe*, 1, 572. For a Latrobe schematic sketch of the order see BHL to Charles Willson Peale, April 18, 1806, see Van Horne and Formwalt, *Correspondence of Latrobe*, 2, 215.

of the *National Intelligencer*: "On entering, the eye catches at once, the first vaulted vestibule, opening by a lofty arch into the staircase; beyond the staircase, the octagon vestibule of the offices with its octangular vaulted ceiling above, the fluted dome of the stairs, supported by 8 columns in pairs between the angle piers, and through the intercolumniations, the hemispherical dome of the vestibule of the Hall of Representatives, enriched with circular pannels and roses. All this scenery is lighted by the lanthorns of the two domes."[63] What Latrobe did not mention, possibly to avoid calling attention to the details and offending Jefferson, is that throughout this complex he used paired Attic columns (Figure 19).

In deciding to decorate these spaces with the Attic, Latrobe also may have been encouraged by a long-standing architectural protocol that Stuart and Revett had confirmed as being Greek in origin. With regard to the sequence of the orders when stacked, as on the Arch of Theseus at Athens, to use their example, the Ionic was to stand above the Doric, the Corinthian above the Ionic, and only the Corinthian order could sit above another Corinthian column.[64] The floor of the House with its colossal order was in fact somewhat lower than the vestibule with its reduced columns. Access between the two was by a short intervening flight of steps, which only confirmed the idea of alluding here to sequence and superimposition. In this instance it would appear that Latrobe not only accepted expeditiously the disparaging association between the Corinthian and the Attic, but simultaneously he also took advantage of their distinct differences in appearance.

On examination it also becomes clear that the Attic capitals used in the vestibule and stairwell differ ever so slightly from the originals illustrated in the *Antiquities of Athens*. In the upper register, between the elongated and slender waterleaves, the engraving shows narrow, but empty, interstices. Into these gaps Latrobe had inserted another plant form, a narrow stem with a small leaf or flower at the end. Although this appears as a gesture that personalized the design, what is striking is that virtually the same feature is also found on a Coade version, whether in the firm's engraved catalog or on the capital that he previously used for Ashdown, his English country house. But even the introduction of this slight enhancing variant, Latrobe probably saw as a Grecianizing gesture. To his mind the Greeks, in tune with democratic freedom, had encouraged and permitted individual invention and originality, whereas the Romans and their later admirers, notably the Palladians, had limited and demeaned architecture. As he once

---

[63] Benjamin Henry Latrobe, "Letter to the Editor," *National Intelligencer*, November 22, 1807, reprinted in Van Horne and Formwalt, *Correspondence of Latrobe*, 2, 505. Earlier, without going into any excessive detail, such as identifying the order, the room also is mentioned in the report of April 4, 1803; see Van Horne and Formwalt, *Correspondence of Latrobe*, I, 275–76. Initially, as a c. 1805 drawing (LC-USZ62-13244) indicates, he seems to have introduced columns on only one side of the stairwell.

[64] On this point see Riou, *Grecian Orders*, 48.

Figure 19. Benjamin Henry Latrobe, small rotunda adjoining House of Representatives, 1806–07.

Office of the Architect of the Capitol.

informed Lenthall, they had "endeavored to establish fixed rules for the most minute parts of the orders. The Greeks knew of no such rules, but having established *general* proportions and laws of form and arrangement, all matters of detail were left to the talent and taste of individual architects. This is amply proved in all their best buildings."[65]

---

[65] BHL to John Lenthall, August 5, 1804: Van Horne and Formwalt, *Correspondence of Latrobe*, 1, 527–28.

6

Latrobe and the Attic Outside Washington

— A Capital Problem —

Despite these various setbacks in giving prominence to the Attic order at the Capitol, Latrobe's interest in the Tower of the Winds and its columns remained undiminished. At the Bank of Pennsylvania, with which he was involved in Philadelphia from 1798 to 1807, he applied a marble roof, which it has been suggested was inspired by the similar covering on the Tower.[66] And at Dickinson College in Carlisle, Pennsylvania, on a project begun in 1803, about two years later, atop the lantern on the college's roof he placed a vane that imitated the triton that had stood atop the Tower, though, maintaining the marine reference, he did transform the triton into a mermaid.[67] With regard to the Attic order itself, outside of the Capitol its most prominent proposed use was in some of the designs Latrobe offered for his other major monumental commission of this first decade, the cathedral for the Catholic diocese of Baltimore, seat of the first Bishopric in America.

The initial design for the Minor Basilica of the Assumption of the Blessed Virgin Mary that he presented to Bishop John Carroll was Gothic and the second design was Roman. The third and fourth proposals are now lost but they seem to have been further variants on the Roman. But the fifth was different. Writing to his patron of his own satisfaction with this latest design, February 26, 1806, Latrobe observed that it was "a satisfaction I have never yet enjoyed since our last *melting down* of the original plan in the Roman taste. The thing is now just what I wish it."[68] A March 6, 1806, drawing clearly demonstrates that a major component of this latest design was the extensive use of the Attic order (Figure 20).[69] Six Attic columns support the cathedral's portico and others are used extensively on the interior, notably at the apsidal end. Regretfully, neither this plan, nor a similar sixth design found favor with the diocese and in early 1808 there followed a seventh proposal in which the portico remained Attic (Figure 21), but the apsidal columns had been changed to the Ionic of the Erechtheum as illustrated in volume two, 1787, of the *Antiquities of Athens*.[70] Finally, as completed in 1821, all the requisite capitals for the Cathedral, exterior and interior, were carved in this same Ionic order, thus making the building, even if devoid of Attic capitals, a distinct and major

---

[66] For the Bank, see Cohen and Brownell, *Drawings of Latrobe*, 1, 68, 188–227.

[67] For the vane and Latrobe's concern with location and the prevailing local winds, recalling the placement of the original Tower, see Paul F. Norton, "Latrobe and Old West at Dickinson College," Art Bulletin 33 (1951):128–29, 130. Also see Cohen and Brownell, *Drawings of Latrobe*, 2, 427.

[68] BHL to John Carroll, February 26, 1806: Van Horne and Formwalt, *Correspondence of Latrobe*, 2, 194–95. Carroll's own initial interest was in the Corinthian: see Cohen and Brownell, *Drawings of Latrobe*, 2, 432; and generally for the Cathedral, 431–91; Hamlin, *Latrobe*, 232–52; and Mary E. Hayward and Frank R. Shivers Jr., eds., *The Architecture of Baltimore: An Illustrated History* (Baltimore: Johns Hopkins University Press, 2004), 70–3.

[69] Cohen and Brownell, *Drawings of Latrobe*, 2, 438–40, 469–78..

[70] For this Ionic order, see Stuart and Revett, *Antiquities of Athens*, 2, chapter 2, 20 and pl. 5; and for Latrobe's fifth, sixth, with its slight variants on the fifth, and seventh designs, *Drawings of Latrobe*, 2, 478–88.

Figure 20. Benjamin Henry Latrobe, *Baltimore Cathedral, longitudinal section looking north*, after 6 March 1806 and before 25 May 1807.

Figure 21. Benjamin Henry Latrobe, *Section of the Cathedral of Baltimore from west to east*, 1808. Collection, Archdiocese of Baltimore.

example of the Greek Revival in America, a posthumous testimonial—he had died the previous year—to Latrobe's efforts at naturalizing this style in his adopted land.

Having dispensed with the idea of installing Attic capitals at the cathedral, Latrobe never did succeed in including the order as a major element into any other project of architectural prominence. This is not to imply that he entirely forsook the order, only that he was unsuccessful.[71] Indeed, in the summer of 1815 Latrobe sought to introduce the Attic on yet another Baltimore project, the Exchange, a vast commercial building that was to include, according to a July 16 memorandum he drafted, a federal customs house, warehouses, insurance companies, brokers' offices, a coffee house, and at the center a great domed Exchange Hall. As he was still resident in Washington, in order to facilitate his work he went into a contentious partnership with Maximillian Godefroy, a local architect whom he had befriended, a gesture that also was intended to remove his accomplished colleague from vying for the same commission.[72] In late August or early the next month, Latrobe forwarded two drawings for the project, an elevation (Figure 22) and a section (Figure 23), to an encouraging friend, Robert Goodloe Harper, a member of the Exchange's newly formed Board of Trustees.[73] Although the drafting is now attributed to Latrobe, the drawings presumably represented a collaborative conceptual effort by the partners.

In this initial design, the stark and simple façades recall work by the revolutionary generation of French architecture and undoubtedly owe much to Godefroy, a Parisian with some training as a civil engineer who arrived in America as a Napoleonic exile in 1805.[74] Whatever Latrobe's contribution was, it assuredly included the extensive use of the Attic order.[75] To afford

---

[71] For example, Fazio and Snadon, without documentation, suggest that the order was introduced in the drawing room of the Markoe House, Philadelphia, 1807–10; Fazio and Snadon, *Domestic Architecture of Latrobe*, 347.

[72] See Hamlin, *Latrobe*, 486–97; and Robert L. Alexander, *The Architecture of Maximillian Godefroy* (Baltimore: Johns Hopkins University Press, 1974), 114–18.

[73] Cohen and Brownell, *Drawings of Latrobe*, 2, 637–39, 647–50. Also see Hayward and Shivers, *Architecture of Baltimore*, 75–79, who take no notice of the Attic order.

[74] For references to such sources, see Cohen and Brownell, *Drawings of Latrobe*, 2, 646–47; and more fully, Alexander, *Godefroy*, 118–19 and passim. Also see Antoinette J. Lee, *Architects to the Nation: The Rise and Decline of the Sponsoring Architect's Office* (New York: Oxford University Press, 2000), 15–17.

[75] Influenced perhaps by Latrobe, though on a minor scale, earlier, 1813–15, Godefroy had used such capitals for the Robert William Smith tomb at First Presbyterian Church. Again as a lesser element, he proposed using the order for the organ loft at the Baltimore Unitarian Church, 1817–18, a project on which Latrobe was involved in the preliminary drawings. However, reflecting perhaps his French origins and Napoleon's conquest of Egypt, Godefroy regarded the order not as Greek, but as Egyptian. For these projects and his opinions on the order's origins, see Alexander, *Godefroy*, 30–31, 90–92, 132–56, 224–225. To judge from a sectional drawing, dated February 21, 1817, Latrobe had proposed using either the Attic or Corinthian order for the Unitarian Church's upper gallery, but the detail on the drawing is too slight to allow a specific identification, though very likely he would have intended the former; for the drawing and Latrobe's involvement with this project generally, see Cohen and Brownell, *Drawings of Latrobe*, 2, 681–86.

— A Capital Problem —

Figure 22. Benjamin Henry Latrobe, *Baltimore Exchange, first design transverse section, looking west*, late August to early September 1815. Courtesy of the Maryland Historical Society, Item ID# 2017-167.

Figure 23. Benjamin Henry Latrobe, *Baltimore Exchange, first design, East (Gay Street) elevation*, late August to early September 1815. Courtesy of the Maryland Historical Society, Item ID# 2017-167.

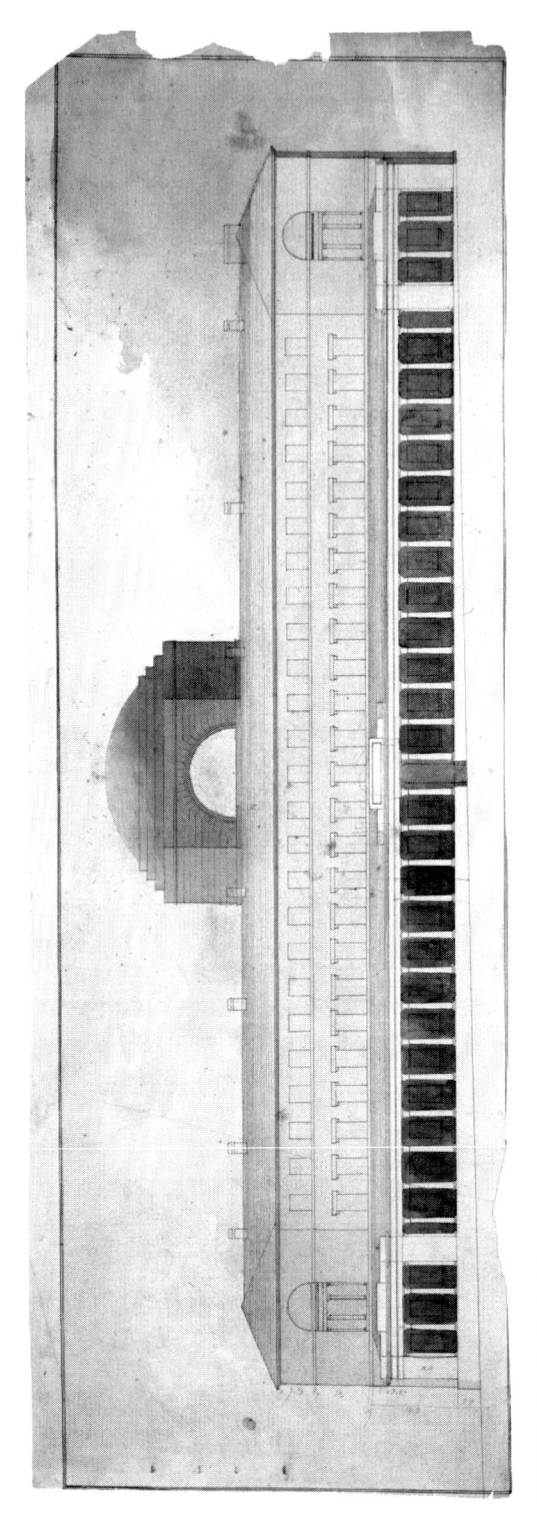

shelter to the passing populace, on the east side of the building running along but elevated slightly above street level, there was a ground-story colonnade about 250 feet long and marked by thirty columns, each capped with Attic capitals. Entry to this walkway was either at the unobtrusive center or the ends. The Exchange's formal entrance was at the south end, where the visitor was welcomed into a courtyard ringed on three sides by yet another Attic colonnade, Exchange Walk. Finally at the north end an enclosed courtyard had similar colonnades along its east and west sides. But this was not the design that won the commission, for, as Godefroy indicated to his partner, with its markedly downward slope the site was not especially suitable to the unyielding classical elevation they proposed. When they were finally awarded the contract in February 1816, in both plan and appearance their proposal for the building had been completely transformed and it was built with façades that entirely omitted the public colonnades and there is no indication that the Attic capital was retained anywhere else, neither on the exterior or interior.[76]

---

[76] See Cohen and Brownell, *Drawings of Latrobe*, 2, 639–47, 651–58. Disputes over the commission also led to a rupture in the friendship between Latrobe and Godefroy, for which see Alexander, *Godefroy*, 205–06.

7

Latrobe Returns to the Capitol

— A Capital Problem —

Nor did Latrobe replicate the Attic order as a major component during his second campaign at the United States Capitol, to which he had returned as architect by appointment of President James Madison in April 1815, just prior to his getting involved with the Baltimore Exchange. However, again as a lesser decorative element, he did succeed in installing a purposefully devised variant on the Attic capital in a newly contrived space. Inspecting the fire-damaged building Latrobe found that the north wing had suffered the most destruction and would require substantial rebuilding.[77] Of the spaces there only the vestibule entrance on the ground floor with its distinctive corncob capitals, which had been sculpted to his design, survived in any preservable form. By contrast, both the Supreme Court and Senate chambers were damaged beyond usefulness. For the Senate, however, the catastrophe proved to be somewhat advantageous. With the expansion of the Union, an opportunity now was provided to enlarge their hall in order to accommodate several newly admitted states and even some anticipated admissions. Besides remaining in their same essential locations, it also was decided that as rebuilt each would retain its previous architectural style; the Supreme Court was to remain Doric and the Senate directly above, like Baltimore cathedral, was to use the Grecian Ionic of the Erechtheum.

Another great loss in the north wing was the space that prior to the fire had enclosed "the great Staircase." Located just off the central rotunda, from the building's beginnings this handsome stairwell had served as a major circulation point between the ground and principal floors. It was as Latrobe informed Jefferson, November 5, 1816, "one of the most remarkable parts of the Capitol." However, rather than repairing or recreating the damaged stairs, Latrobe determined to make the space distinctly his own. On the same north–south central axis he would create a pendant to the Attic vestibule that he had earlier installed between the central dome and the House of Representatives. As he further informed Jefferson, this new passageway was to be a

> Vestibule, in the Center of which a circular Colonnade will support a dome for the purpose of admitting light. The Columns of this Rotunda, 16 in number, must be more slender than the Ionic order will admit, and ought not to be of the Corinthian, because the Chamber itself is only of the Ionic order. I have therefore composed a Capital of the Leaves and flowers of the Tobacco plant, which has an intermediate effect approaching the character of the Corinthian order, and retained the simplicity of the Attic Column of the Clepsydra, or Temple of the Winds.[78]

---

[77] For Latrobe's second campaign, see Cohen and Brownell, *Drawings of Latrobe*, 577–637; Hamlin, 438–56; and Allen, *History of the Capitol*, 97–123.

[78] Van Horne and Formwalt, *Correspondence of Latrobe*, 3, 822–24. Also see Cohen and Brownell, *Drawings of Latrobe*, 2, 583–84, 602–03.

A drawing of this new capital was included in the letter's margin (Figure 24). Some months later he also sent Jefferson an actual model of this invention (Figure 25).[79]

Although, as Latrobe observed, this new order was formally derived from the Attic, it also reflects yet another design issue that was being debated within the context of the Greek Revival, that of the legitimacy of creating national orders. Taking up the challenge, during his first turn as the nation's architect Latrobe had created the aforementioned corncob order, which derived from Egyptian precedents, as well as a dwarf order, whose capitals featured stylized magnolia flowers and leafs. This latter, another loss in the 1814 fire, had provided a screen for select guests who were invited to observe the Senate's proceedings from a private gallery at the rear, just above the chamber's main entrance. Although Latrobe argued for the inclusion of his latest creation by referring to theories of proportion that discouraged any use of the Corinthian in the new vestibule, his remarks on the protocols that prevailed when the Corinthian and Ionic were in close proximity seem somewhat self-serving. As already noted, according to architectural theory the Corinthian could legitimately stand above the Ionic order, but such a rule became ambiguous when the two came into proximity in a processional scheme. Other than niches for paintings and sculpture, Latrobe intended the large central rotunda of the Capitol to be devoid of any orders, but the sequential relationship between the orders in the small vestibule and those embellishing the larger Ionic Senate chamber was problematic. Although decidedly round like the Attic, like the Corinthian this new order had a third register comprised principally of tobacco flowers. However, as he had informed Jefferson, in place of the pronounced volutes that squared the circle on the Corinthian, at all four corners he included an unobtrusive curling tobacco leaf that presses gently against the abacus above.[80] Both in its proportions and originality, hovering as it does between the Corinthian and Attic, the tobacco order was an attempt to compromise with antiquity and yet to legitimately create within its lingering legacy.

Returning to Latrobe's preference for the orthodox form of the Attic, a final and easily overlooked, even if ubiquitous usage at the Capitol can be identified. As has been seen, as much as he sought futilely to introduce the capitals as part of a colossal order their actual presence had been confined to a secondary and subsidiary area. On a still lesser scale, in offices scattered throughout the building, dwarf Attic columns also were incorporated into several chimneypieces (Figure

---

[79] See BHL to Jefferson, June 28, 1817, Van Horne and Formwalt, *Correspondence of Latrobe*, 3, 906, also 824, n. 4.

[80] See the discussion of the vestibule and its tobacco capitals in Cohen and Brownell, *Drawings of Latrobe*, 2, 583–84, 602–04.

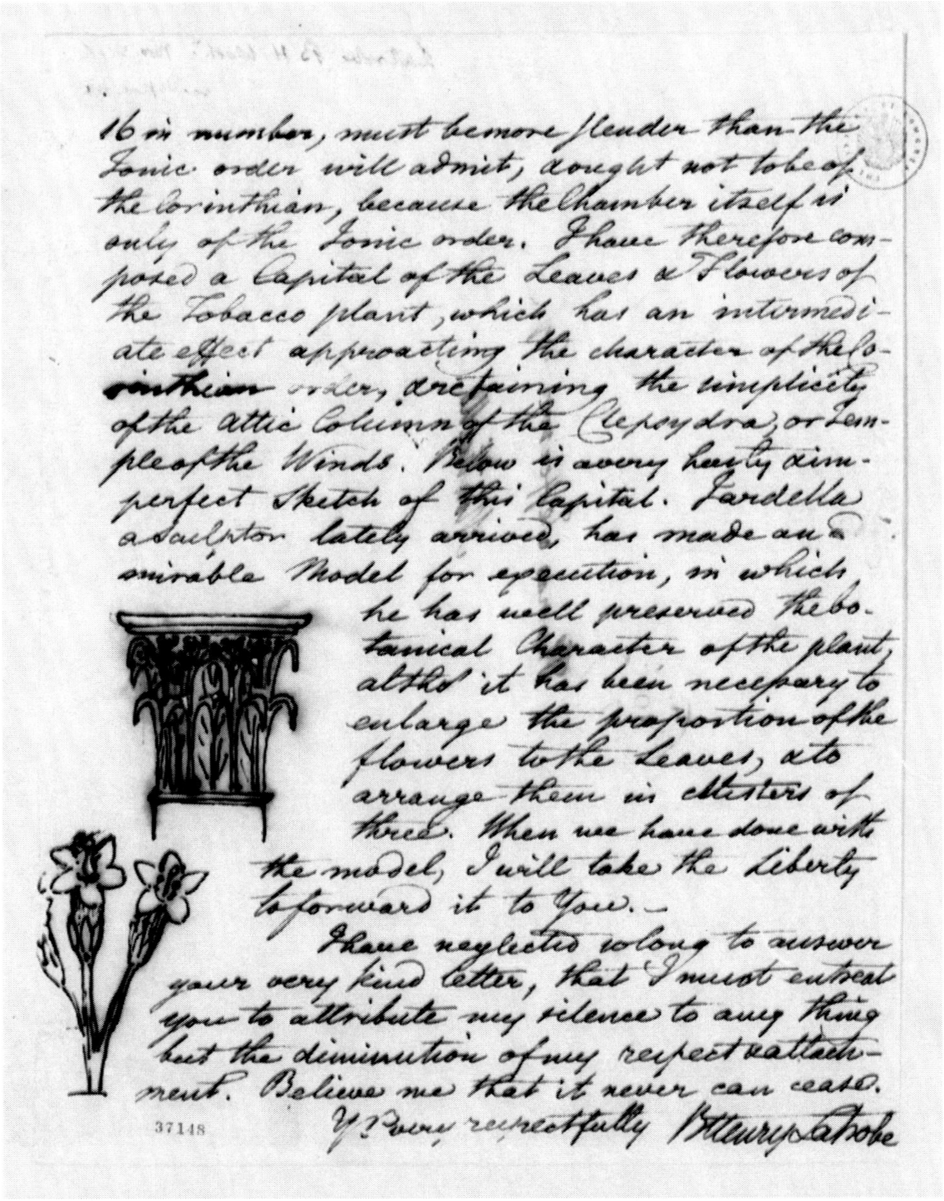

16 in number, must be more slender than the Ionic order will admit, & ought not to be of the Corinthian, because the Chamber itself is only of the Ionic order. I have therefore composed a Capital of the Leaves & Flowers of the Tobacco plant, which has an intermediate effect approaching the character of the Corinthian order, & retaining the simplicity of the attic Column of the Clepsydra, or Temple of the Winds. Below is a very hasty & imperfect Sketch of this Capital. Jardella a Sculptor lately arrived, has made an admirable Model for execution, in which he has well preserved the botanical Character of the plant, altho' it has been necessary to enlarge the proportion of the flowers to the Leaves, & to arrange them in clusters of three. When we have done with the model, I will take the liberty to forward it to You.—

I have neglected so long to answer your very kind letter, that I must entreat you to attribute my silence to any thing but the diminution of my respect & attachment. Believe me that it never can cease.

Y? very respectfully B Henry Latrobe

Figure 24. Benjamin Henry Latrobe to Thomas Jefferson, November 5, 1816.
The Thomas Jefferson Papers, Library of Congress.

Figure 25. Francisco Iardella, after design of Benjamin Henry Latrobe, example of Tobacco Leaf Capital, 1817, sent to Thomas Jefferson at Monticello.

Thomas Jefferson Foundation, Inc., Charlottesville, VA.

— A Capital Problem —

Figure 26.   Mantel, Office of the Sergeant at Arms, US Capitol, after 1814, destroyed 1898.
From Glenn Brown, *History of the United States Capitol* (Washington, DC: U.S. Government Printing Office, 1900–03).

26). Between 1807 and 1809 Latrobe is know to have ordered numbers of fireplaces from a favored supplier, the Traquair's Philadelphia marble yard, but nothing specifically is know of their appearance other than that Andrei and Franzoni were involved with their designs, not all of which included Attic elements.[81] Destined at the Capitol for the House and Senate chambers, committee

---

[81] Individually, the fireplaces are undocumented, but for further information on them, see Van Horne and Formwalt, *Correspondence of Latrobe*, 2, 566, 577, 708–09, 711, 759, 761; Glenn Brown, *History of the United States Capitol* (Washington, DC: U. S. Government Printing Office, 1900–03), 1, 56–57, pls. 75, 76, 107; and Allen, *History of the Capitol*, 71, 74, 120, 137.

rooms and offices, several chimney pieces were installed well prior to the War of 1812, but correspondence with the marble yard in 1816 indicates that following the cessation of hostilities in 1814 and with Latrobe's subsequent return to the building the next year, mantles were still being ordered, whereas others, long ago completed and crated, were finally paid for and dispatched.[82] None seem to have arrived prior to November 1817, by which time Latrobe was terminating his service as Surveyor, which led to their installation by his successor, Charles Bulfinch.[83] Fireplaces with Attic columns are known today in at least eleven offices, though it remains uncertain as to which architect they owe their particular placement.[84]

---

[82] A number of these chimneypieces were apparently destined for the President's House, with whose restoration from wartime fire damage Latrobe also became involved at the behest of President Madison and his wife, Dolley, see Hamlin, *Latrobe*, 300–04; Margaret Brown Klapthor, "Benjamin Latrobe and Dolley Madison Decorate the White House 1809–1811," *Contributions from the Museum of History and Technology, Smithsonian Institution*, 49 (1965): 155–64; and William Seale, *The President's House, A History* (Washington, DC: White House Historical Association with the cooperation of the National Geographic Society, 1986), 1, 122–26.

[83] See *Documentary History of the Construction and Development of the United States Capitol Building and Grounds* (58th Congress, 2nd session, 1904; House report 646, Washington, DC: U.S. Government Printing Office), 201; Van Horne and Formwalt, *Correspondence of Latrobe*, 3, 836–37; and Allen, *History of the Capitol*, 120, 131.

[84] See *Compilation of Works of Art and Other Objects in the United States Capitol* (88th Congress, 2nd session, 1965; House document 362, Washington, DC: U.S. Government Printing Office), 333–37; *Art in the United States Capitol* (91st Congress, 2nd session, 1976; House document 91-368, Washington, DC: U.S. Government Printing Office), 382–85; and a pamphlet, *The U.S. Senate Republican Leader's Suite* (Senate Publication 107-40, Washington, DC: U.S. Government Printing Office).

8

William Nichols and Robert Mills: Taking the Attic Order South

— A Capital Problem —

Regardless of his contribution to the Capitol's design and construction, it was apparently either his dilatoriness in completing the rebuilding or, as Latrobe preferred to believe, the jealousy and enmity of other architects and political figures that forced him to resign the Surveyorship on November 20, 1817. As he wrote President Monroe, given the choice between "resignation and the sacrifice of all self respect," he chose the former.[85] Three years later, while residing in New Orleans, he died, but the Capitol remained and continues to be respected as his greatest monument. What is striking about his successors, whether Charles Bulfinch who most immediately worked toward completing his plans or, after midcentury, Thomas Ustick Walter who expanded the Capitol well beyond anything he might have imagined, is that each retained respect for Latrobe's general design and detailing. Curiously, a marker of this continuing esteem, notably for Latrobe's attempts at introducing Greek notes into the building, was, as shall be seen, a lingering use of the Attic order.

Most immediately, however, and well away from Washington, Latrobe's former student William Strickland used Attic capitals in Philadelphia. Under his guidance from 1801, when he entered an apprenticeship, until 1805 or 1807, it is evident that Latrobe was critical to Strickland's stylistic development.[86] Certainly it was Latrobe who introduced him to the *Antiquities of Athens*, on whose plates he regularly relied throughout his professional life.[87] Indeed, in an 1818 Philadelphia competition for the Second Bank of the United States, which requested a "chaste imitation of Grecian Architecture," Strickland's winning entry, a close copy of the Parthenon as published in the second volume of *Antiquities of Athens*, was selected over those, among others, of his onetime fellow student Robert Mills and their common master, though

---

[85] *Correspondence of Latrobe*, 3, 968–69.

[86] For Latrobe and Strickland, see Van Horne and Formwalt, *Correspondence of Latrobe*, 1, 256–57; and for Latrobe's office practices generally, see Fazio and Snadon, *Domestic Architecture of Latrobe*, 185–208.

[87] As Strickland is reputed to have told his own students, "the student of Architecture need go no further than the *Antiquities of Athens* as a basis for design": Agnes Addison Gilchrist, *William Strickland, Architect and Engineer, 1788–1854* (Philadelphia: University of Pennsylvania Press, 1950), 31. Reflecting this retained as well as revived interest there is J.B. Papworth's 1822 remark, which even if directed to England was just as applicable to America, that the contents of the *Antiquities of Athens* are "over and over again copied for any and every purpose, and with them the public are satisfied": J.B. Papworth, "Hints on Ornamental Gardening," *Repository of Arts* (December, 1822), as quoted in Dora Wiebenson, *Sources of Greek Revival Architecture* (London: 1969), 73–74. Another stimulus or reinforcement for Greek architecture would have come from the travel volumes of an English traveler, Edward Dodwell; *A Classical and Topographic Tour through Greece, During the Years 1801, 1805, and 1806* (London: Rodwell & Martin, 1819), 1, 373–74, who gives extensive coverage to the Tower and previous representations; and his *View in Greece* (London: Rodwell and Martin, 1821). The earlier book, for example, had a great impact on the South Carolinian John Izard Middleton, sometimes regarded as America's first classical archaeologist, who excavated in Italy 1807–09, and 1818–23, and who despite his intentions never made it to Greece; for which, see *The Roman Remains: John Izard Middleton's Visual Souvenirs of 1820-23 with Additional Views in Italy, France and Switzerland*, eds. Charles R. Mack and Lynn Robertson (Columbia, SC: University of South Carolina Press, 1997).

Latrobe would claim that there were uncomfortably striking similarities between the winning design and his own proposal.[88]

It was in 1820, still in Philadelphia, that Strickland turned to the Attic, including it on the façade of the second Chestnut Street Theatre.[89] Latrobe's original edifice had burned in April and by May Strickland was offering proposals for the rebuilding. Discarding the Tuscan doorway of his initial drawing, the theatre as built had a rusticated ground floor with arched openings and above a portico of four Temple of the Winds columns in antis, with the facing pilasters similarly decorated (Figure 27). Completed in this manner in 1822, the capitals were carved in Italy due to the enduring scarcity of skilled craftsmen that had previously plagued his mentor. Short lived, Strickland's theatre was demolished in 1856.

To return to the nation's capital, Bulfinch's appointment as Architect to the Capitol became effective in January just after Latrobe's resignation; he would remain in that office until his death in 1829.[90] Working initially as a gentleman amateur, his work on the Massachusetts state house demonstrates that he was not an especial admirer of Greek architecture. He preferred instead English work of a more decidedly Roman bent, notably that of the Adam brothers and William Chambers, examples of which he had seen when traveling abroad as a young man.[91] In approaching the Capitol, however, Bulfinch saw his primary task as the fulfillment of Latrobe's plans. Writing to his wife immediately after taking office, he observed:

> I feel the responsibility resting on me, and should have no resolution to proceed if the work was not so far commenced as to make it necessary to follow the plans already prepared for the wings; as to the centre building, a general conformity to the other parts must be maintained. I shall not have credit for invention, but must be content to follow in the prescribed path.[92]

One of Bulfinch's major contributions was new quarters for the Library of Congress, which prior to the 1814 fire had been located in the Senate wing, but

---

[88] For this competition and the dispute over originality, see Gilchrist, *Strickland*, 53–58; and Cohen and Brownell, *Drawings of Latrobe*, 2, 708–36

[89] See Gilchrist, *Strickland*, 35, 60–61, who refers to the order as Corinthian; and Irwin R. Glazer, *Philadelphia Theatres, A Pictorial Architectural History* (Philadelphia: Dover Publications, 1994), xii–xiv.

[90] For Bulfinch at the Capitol, see Kirker, *Bulfinch*, 321–33; Pamela Scott, "Charles Bulfinch, Well-Connected, Refined Gentleman Architect," in Kennon, *Designing and Decorating a National Icon*, 56–84; and Allen, *History of the Capitol*, 125–67.

[91] For the early development of Bulfinch's style and his earlier Grecian essays, see Haferterpe and O'Gorman, *American Architects*, 92–107.

[92] Bulfinch to Hannah Bulfinch, January 7, [1818]: *The Life and Letters of Charles Bulfinch, Architect*, ed. Ellen Susan Bulfinch (Boston: Houghton, Mifflin, 1896), 214. Latrobe and Bulfinch apparently never met, but on March 25, 1807, in a very cordial letter, Latrobe sought Bulfinch's assistance with regard to the ceiling painting of the House: Van Horne and Formwalt, *Correspondence of Latrobe*, 2, 398–99.

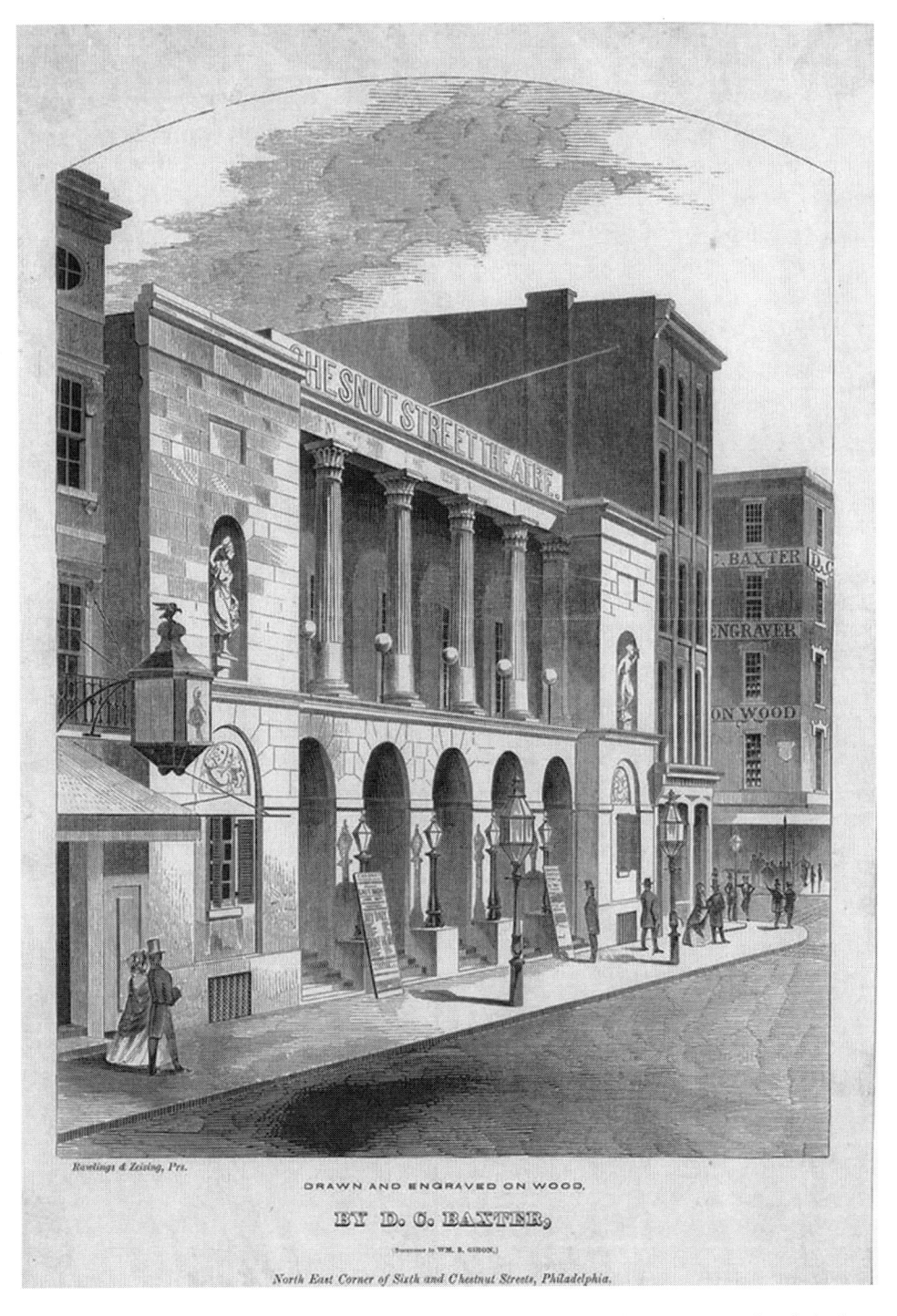

Figure 27. William Strickland, *Chestnut Street Theatre*, Philadelphia, 1820–22, demolished 1856.

Wood engraving by D.G. Baxter.

whose space in the aftermath was given over to committees and offices. Toward the end of his term as Surveyor, Latrobe had proposed that a new wing be added to the Capitol, an extension to the east from the central section. Here, on the principal floor just behind a new western façade, his drawings indicate that he intended to locate a new reading room. With his removal, however, the actual task of designing and supervising construction of this addition fell to Bulfinch as his successor. Regardless of Latrobe's original intentions, apparently to decorate the chamber in the Egyptian style, a recollection perhaps of the great library at Alexandria, Bulfinch's decision was to transform the library into something of a salute to his recently deceased predecessor, by decorating it with Attic columns on a scale that his predecessor had never managed to achieve.

On leaving the central rotunda, the visitor passed through a short corridor whose Ionic colonnade screened the new wing's main stairwell and came directly to a doorway framed by paired and attached Attic columns (Figure 28).[93] The appearance of the interior beyond, which opened for service in the summer of 1824, is known only from an 1832 drawing by Alexander Jackson Davis, which was subsequently transformed into a more finished work with figures by Stephen H. Gilmer, seemingly a study for what appears to be an unpublished lithograph (Figure 29),[94] but it is also concisely described in Robert Mill's 1834 *Guide to the Capitol*:

> At the entrance from the rotunda are two stone columns in advance, with capitals corresponding with those in the octagon tower at Athens; and immediately opposite, fronting the outlet into the western colonnade are two similar columns in advance. On each side of the central entrance, and extending the whole length of the room are a series of alcoves, ornamented in front with fluted pilasters, which, with their entablatures, support two galleries.[95]

---

[93] These columns apparently no longer survive, but were noted and illustrated by Glenn Brown, *History of the Capitol*, 2, pl. 104. As there is no indication of them in any of the floor plans, it is also conceivable that they were not original to this location, but assuming they survived the fire that destroyed Bulfinch's congressional library in 1851, they were subsequently moved there or were introduced at some other time.

[94] For the initial drawing, see Roger Hale Newton, "Bulfinch's Design for the Library of Congress," *Art Bulletin*, 23 (1941): 221–22. For the 1823 purchase order for the marble blocks for the four free-standing columns and their subsequent carving, see Allen, *History of the Capitol*, 2, pl. 104. The framing and finish of the drawing suggests that it was prepared for engraving or lithography. For another Davis drawing, apparently a preparatory study, see Roger Hale Newton, "Bulfinch's Design for the Library of Congress," *Art Bulletin* 23 (1941): 221–22. For the purchase order for the columns see Allen, *History of the Capitol*, 147.

[95] Robert Mills, *Guide to the Capitol of the United States* (Washington, DC, 1934), 47. For a fuller description of the room that also identifies these columns, see an article sometimes attributed to Edgar Allan Poe, "The Capitol at Washington," *Burton's Gentleman's Magazine* (November 1839): 233.

Figure 28. Charles Bulfinch, Entrance, Library of Congress, United States Capitol, 1818–24.

From Glenn Brown, *History of the United States Capitol* (Washington, DC: U.S. Government Printing Office, 1900–03).

Figure 29. Charles Bulfinch, *Congress Library. Capitol. Washington*, as drawn by Alexander Jackson Davis, 1832.

I.N. Phelps Stokes Collection, Miriam and Ira D. Wallach Division of Art, Prints and Photographs, The New York Public Library, New York Astor, Lenox, and Tilden Foundations.

— A Capital Problem —

As the Davis drawing further confirms, these pilasters and columns were all Attic in design.[96]

In 1828, in the Senate chamber, yet again Bulfinch paid tribute to Latrobe by means of the Attic order, though it came at a cost to his predecessor's work. Removing the awkwardly situated public gallery that Latrobe had installed with great difficulty at the front of the rebuilt Senate, he replaced the needed accommodation with a new visitors' balcony that followed the Chamber's curved rear wall and rested on a series of slender cast-iron columns detailed in the same Attic order.[97] Eventually, taken down in 1859, when the room was converted for use by the Supreme Court, their appearance is known from several paintings and prints that depict Senate debates during the intervening years and which subsequently served as a key source when, in 1976, what is now the old Senate chamber was restored to an earlier appearance (Figure 30).[98]

By the time Bulfinch left the Capitol in 1829 the Greek Revival can be said to have achieved real prominence in American architecture, especially with regard to governmental and civic structures. An impact on domestic designs would follow. Undoubtedly, the association of the style with Athenian democracy was a force for its success, but its detached freshness also must have been a factor. Unlike the Roman style, which through the centuries had become linked to systems of secular and religious authoritarianism, the Greek had little recent

---

[96] As much as he might have admired Latrobe's Attic capitals, Bulfinch also found it necessary to remove two. Writing to his wife, January 7, 1818, he observed that he found Latrobe's "stile is calculated for display in the greater parts, but I think his staircases in general are crowded, and not easy of access, and the passages intricate and dark. Indeed the whole interior, except the two great rooms, has a sombre appearance"; *Life and Letters of Bulfinch*, 213–14. In seeking to relieve this gloom by opening the building to more natural light, he made a significant alteration to the lightwell with its adjoining staircase that led from the ground floor to the House vestibule above, the only places in the Capitol where in fact Latrobe had succeeded in introducing the Attic order. In creating a more commodious space he introduced a monumental staircase that opened directly onto the lightwell, a change that necessitated the removal of the pair of columns on the south side. The original configuration is seen in an 1804 Latrobe drawing of the south wing; Cohen and Brownell, *Drawings of Latrobe*, 2, 372–74, as well as in a plan, 1817, from his second campaign that shows the reconfigured House chamber, Pamela Scott, *Temple of Liberty* (New York: Oxford University Press, 1995), 129, pl. 155. The subsequent arrangement presents itself in two Alexander Jackson Davis floor plans, 1832–34, for which, see Scott, *Temple of Liberty*, 131, pls. 172, 173. For a view of the alteration, see Allen, *History of the Capitol*, 166.
[97] See Allen, *History of the Capitol*, 163–64.
[98] For example, Peter F. Rothermel, *The United States Senate, A.D. 1850*, known in an 1855 Robert Whitechurch engraving, and an 1851 painting by G.F.L. Healy, for which see Frederick Voss, "Webster Replying to Hayne: George Healy and the Economics of History Paintings," *American Art* 15 no. 3 (2001), 34–53.

Figure 30. Charles Bulfinch, Capital on support columns, Old Senate Chamber, 1828, removed 1859, and recreated for 1976 restoration.

architectural history and was thus largely devoid of such despotic links.[99] Consequently, in the United States, it quickly became the preferred architectural language for institutions representing republicanism and democracy.

---

[99] In the advert that accompanied the second volume of the *Antiquities of Athens*, 1787, ii, it was observed "The present Volume will treat of Buildings, erected while the Athenians were a free people, chiefly during the administration of that great statesman Pericles." There has been some speculation that American sympathy for the Greek revolt against the Turks, 1821–30, also had an impact on the revival, but as the beginnings of a Grecian taste well antedate that uprising the evidence is that it was more a momentary stimulation then a lasting concern and had thus only a minor role: see Robert K. Sutton, *Americans Interpret the Parthenon, The Progression of Greek Revival Architecture from the East Coast to Oregon, 1800–1850* (Niwot, CO: University Press of Colorado, 1992), 42–44; and Maynard, *Architecture in the United States*, 252–53.

9

Taking the Attic Order Beyond Washington

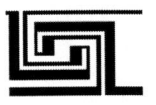

— A Capital Problem —

If Latrobe was largely instrumental in bringing a Grecian taste to America, other architects were essential for its dispersal across the country, the Attic order included. Some practitioners were directly connected to Latrobe, such as his students Strickland and Robert Mills, whereas others were among his devotees, notably Alexander Jackson Davis. William Nichols, working quite independently from this group, also made a significant contribution.

Emigrating around 1800 from his native England directly to North Carolina, Nichols was subsequently active in Alabama and Mississippi, where he designed state capitols. He obtained, as he once informed the governor of Mississippi, "more experience in the construction of State Capitols than any other individual in the Union."[100] Just as the states entering the Union used the national Constitution as the model for their governmental organization, so did Nichols look to the federal Capitol as the architectural paradigm to house each state's legislative needs. He is known to have traveled north in 1817 and 1823, and to judge from his state house designs, very likely visited Washington along the way, but his taste for Greek architecture was very much his own. It seems to have been fostered during his training as a master builder in Britain and flourished with his professional emergence in America. Like others encouraging that style, he too, in a search for authentic detailing, drew heavily on the *Antiquities of Athens*. Yet for Nichol's work on governmental buildings, the example of Latrobe in legitimizing and encouraging the Attic and the other Greek orders must not be discounted.

Recalling Latrobe's reality, however, his use of the Attic order in the state houses was always in a minor key; it never appeared on the exterior or in the larger public spaces where, not unexpectedly, the canonical three always were preferred.[101] In North Carolina, 1820–24, he remodeled an earlier building in Raleigh. By changing the plan to a Greek cross with a dome over the crossing and pedimented porticos on two sides that included attached Ionic columns, he succeeded in giving it a classical guise. Of his interior finishes nothing is known and all was lost in an 1831 fire.[102] That Nichols may have introduced the Attic order there only can be surmised, the evidence being its presence in two of his subsequent state houses.

---

[100] Quoted from C. Ford Peatross, *William Nichols, Architect* (Tuscaloosa, AL: University of Alabama Art Gallery, 1979), 23. Also see John Sanders, "William Nichols," in *Dictionary of North Carolina Biography* (Chapel Hill, NC: University of North Carolina Press, 1979–96), 4, 369–71.

[101] Domestically, however, Nichols did apply a variant on the Attic order, made up only of the water leaves, on interior columns and fireplace supports at Hayes Plantation, Edenton, North Carolina, for which, see Peatross, *Nichols*, 10–11, 36; and Catherine Bishir, "'Serene Servitude to House Building': The Construction of Hayes Plantation, 1814–1817," *North Carolina Historical Review* 68 (1991): 373–403, and for his use of the *Antiquities of Athens*, 380. William Strickland also used such a variant on the ground floor of the Philadelphia Exchange Company, 1832–34; see Gilchrist, *Strickland*, 10, 85.

[102] For this North Carolina state house, see Peatross, *Nichols*, 11–12, 37; and Henry-Russell Hitchcock and William Seale, *Temples of Democracy, The State Capitols of the USA* (New York: Harcourt Brace Jovanovich, 1976), 65–67.

In 1827, apparently having exhausted the professional opportunities available to him in North Carolina, he migrated to Alabama, where shortly after his arrival he was named state architect and set to work on a new state house for Tuscaloosa, 1827–31. In its exterior appearance Nichols's design very much resembled his remodeling in North Carolina. Recalling perhaps Bulfinch's gallery in Latrobe's Senate chamber, Nichols included a colonnade of slender fluted Attic columns to mark the spectators' section in the High Court of Errors and Appeals.[103] In 1833 he moved on and after a brief interlude in New Orleans arrived in Mississippi in 1835, where the next year he was appointed state architect and immediately began planning a new state house in Jackson. Again, the Attic was relegated to the state's highest court (Figure 31), the Supreme Court.[104] In subsequent years Nichols did come to use the Attic order more boldly, but on lesser public projects. Around midcentury, he was the architect for a court house in Yazoo City, whose "Upper or principal story," according to a contemporary account, "is decorated with pilasters, the capitals of which are enriched with leaves, etc., similar to those of the Temple of the Winds at Athens."[105] Finally, just prior to his death in 1853, he designed a new Female Academy for Lexington, Mississippi, whose prominent hexastyle-pedimented portico featured monumental Attic columns.[106]

The uses of the Attic by Robert Mills, who worked under Latrobe from 1802 to 1806, are less certain, but even if all the applications attributed to him are not entirely secure they do nevertheless represent significant uses of the order. In 1821, having been appointed civil and military architect to his native South Carolina, part of Mills's charge was the construction of a series of county courthouses. In all, before departing the state for Washington in 1830, he would do sixteen, and the type of design he favored for several, the pedimented temple front with giant columns, would resonate significantly across the expanding nation. Most frequently, he appears to have used the Doric, and sometimes the Ionic, but in at least one example, in the courthouse in Greenville (Figure 32), erected between 1821 and 1824, subsequently renovated and finally razed a century later, he apparently employed his own variant on the Attic order.[107]

---

[103] See Peatross, *Nichols*, 18, 40; and Hitchcock and Seale, *Temples of Democracy*, 69–70.

[104] See Peatross, *Nichols*, 27–28, 43; and Hitchcock and Seale, *Temples of Democracy*, 76–77

[105] Quoted from Peatross, *Nichols*, 30. Also see Mills Lane, *Architecture of the Old South: Greek Revival and Romantic* (Savannah, GA: Beehive Foundation, 1996), 29.

[106] Razed in 1904. For a photograph and commentary, see Peatross, *Nichols*, 31, 46, 50.

[107] For this otherwise little discussed courthouse, see Blanche Marsh, *Robert Mills; Architect in South Carolina* (Columbia: R. L. Bryan Co., 1970), 142–43; and more extensively, Gene Waddell and Rhodri W. Liscombe, *Robert Mills's Courthouses & Jails* (Easley, SC, Southern Historical Press, 1981), 4, 9, 35, 44–45. For the architect's inventiveness when it came to the orders, see Robert L. Alexander, "The Special Orders of Robert Mills," in *The Documented Image: Visions in Art History*, eds. Gabriel Weisberg and Laurinda Dixon (Syracuse, NY: Syracuse University Press, 1987), 243–56. For more on temple-fronted courthouses and their architectural symbolism, see Michael Kammen, *In the Past Lane: Historical Perspectives in American Culture* (New York: Oxford University Press: 1997), 102–09.

— A Capital Problem —

Figure 31. (a) William Nichols, Supreme Court, Old Mississippi State Capitol, Jackson, Mississippi, 1835–40.

Interior photo by Charlie Brenner.

Figure 31. (b) William Nichols, Supreme Court, Old Mississippi State Capitol, Jackson, Mississippi, 1835–40.

Exterior photo, HABS MISS, 25-JACK, 3-2.

Returning to Mills, his next use of the Attic, although at the United States Capitol, was relatively inconsequential. His move to Washington had been at the behest of the House Committee on Public Buildings. Besides his architectural training with Latrobe, he also had been extensively trained by his mentor as an engineer.[108] It was largely in that capacity that he had been invited to the capitol and his initial federal work included installing sanitary systems in the Capitol and improving the acoustics in the House chamber. In time his larger architectural ambitions came to the fore. Under the patronage of President Andrew Jackson he acquired major commissions in Washington and for federal facilities across the nation, leading him in July 1836, after a self-generated campaign, to a presidential designation as Architect of Public Buildings.

At the Capitol, however, Mills's various ideas for grandiose changes, to the rotunda, for example, came to naught, and his architectural contributions were largely confined to practical renovations, an exception being an unobtrusive public hydrant commissioned by the House and installed in 1834 to

---

[108] For Mills's training as an architect and engineer under Latrobe, see John M. Bryan, *America's First Architect, Robert Mills* (Princeton, NJ: Princeton University Press, 2001), 35–47.

— A Capital Problem —

Figure 32. Robert Mills, County Courthouse, Greenville, South Carolina, 1821–24, demolished 1924.

commemorate the completion of a water supply system to the building (Figure 33). Located on the west front, it was placed between the paired staircases that led to the upper terrace that Bulfinch had designed for access to his recently extended façade. Recalling an ancient stele, the fountain included four dwarf Attic columns, which support an entablature surmounted by an ornamental vase.[109] From the center of this structure water poured forth from a bronze spigot into a bronze urn and the overflow drained into a catch basin. Judging from its appearance, it seems that the columns employed were either surplus, remainders from Latrobe's various fireplaces, or recalling those examples had been carved at that scale specifically for this commission.[110]

Beyond these two projects involving the Attic order, Mills has been associated with two others, though his actual contribution to each remains undefined

---

[109] See Brown, *History of the Capitol*, 1, 72; Allen, *History of the Capitol*, 177–78; Liscombe, *Altogether American*, 176–77; and James M. Goode, *Capital Losses, A Cultural History of Washington's Destroyed Buildings* (Washington, DC, 1979), 303. As Goode notes, in 1887 when Olmstead redesigned the Capitol grounds, the fountain was moved to St. Elizabeth's Hospital, from where it has since disappeared. Often mistakenly thought to be a joint project with the sculptor Hiram Powers, the fountain is now acknowledged to be a work by Mills alone, for which, see Richard P. Wunder, *Hiram Powers, Vermont Sculptor, 1805–1873* (Newark, DE: University of Delaware Press, 1991), 2, 215–16.

[110] Mills writing to William Noland, the Commissioner of Public Buildings, July 9, 1834, noted that the hydrant was to be "made up of old marble work," a reference perhaps to these columns, but just as likely to other parts. I owe this reference to Pamela Scott.

Figure 33. Robert Mills, public hydrant, United States Capitol, Washington, DC, 1834. Wasingtoniana Collection, District of Columbia Public Library.

and even questionable. In 1836, he was approached to design a freestanding library building, the Caroliniana, as it came to be called, which would serve South Carolina College at Columbia, the state capital. Whatever the reason, whether financial exigency or a matter of taste, his extravagant plan for a pedimented Doric portico resting on a rusticated basement and a complex interior centered on the Library Hall, a large domed and colonnaded rotunda, was rejected in favor of a much simpler scheme. Officially opened in May 1840, the library's designer remains unidentified.[111] Given the prestige still attached to the revised project, it was evidently determined that the most suitable and readily available model for the reading room was Bulfinch's recently completed Library of Congress, complete with Attic columns marking the entry vestibule and similar ornamented pilasters at the ends of the bookcases

---

[111] For the library, see Newton, "Bullfinch's Design"; John M. Bryan, *An Architectural History of the South Carolina College, 1801–1855* (Columbia, SC: University of South Carolina Press, 1976), 87–95; Bryan, *America's First Architect*, 268–72; and Liscombe, *Altogether American*, 196–97. Interestingly, in 1802, Mills and Latrobe had both entered the competition for the college's central building, with Mills being one of two architects sharing the prize, though neither winning proposal was ever built: see Bryan, *History of the South Carolina College*, 1–23, 123–25; and Bryan, *America's First Architect*, 22–26.

Figure 34. Attributed to Robert Mills, South Caroliniana Library, Columbia, South Carolina, 1838–40.
University of South Carolina Libraries.

that define the study alcoves, this chamber was eventually recreated in South Carolina (Figure 34). Whether Mills in Washington retained an advisory role in finalizing the library's appearance or if it fell to some anonymous local builder is unknown, but as the Library of Congress interiors were not illustrated, other than in the Davis drawings, both the suggestion of it as a source as well as the necessary documentation must have come from some informed, sympathetic, and conveniently placed intermediary, someone who could provide suitable documentation.

Similarly uncertain is Mills's role, if any, in the rebuilding of The Hermitage, President Jackson's home in Davidson County, Tennessee. Originally built between 1831 and 1834 to the designs of David Hammond, a local Greek Revival architect, the house had burned just months after its completion. Jackson, having looked forward to retirement at the mansion, arranged for a rebuilding by the Nashville carpenters Joseph Reiff and William Hume that very much adhered to the previous floor plan. However, where previously the front portico had rested on ten Doric columns, according to the January 1835 builder's contract, the same number could be repeated or there could be a

"First story of front porch with six columns."[112] As built the six were found to suffice and each was topped by a distinctive adaptation of the Attic capital (Figure 35), taken from plates 22 and 30 of the 1827 edition of Benjamin's *Builder's Companion*. Retaining the round bell form of the original, this version retained the acanthus register at the bottom, but rather than having an upper register of waterleaves the acanthus was repeated above, and all are notably spaced apart.[113]

Mills's actual role in the Hermitage's rebuilding, if any, remains unspecified. The only real evidence for his involvement is the summary remarks of William P. Elliot Jr., a young architect then engaged with him on designs for the new federal Patent Office building in Washington. Not a great admirer of Mills, Elliot parenthetically mentioned him in a diary entry, July 5, 1836, as having been "recently employed by General Jackson to make drawings for the Hermitage."[114] The following November, when lamenting Mill's work habits to Alexander Jackson Davis, he wrote reconfirming this relationship: "Nevertheless he having rebuilt the President's Hermitage, he is the greatest Architect in the U. States in the view of the Old Hero."[115] The practical issues these remarks raise are striking, notably that Mills, having never visited the site only could only have known the Hermitage second hand, through drawings and topographic views that might have been in Jackson's possession, yet it was not unusual for architects to work at such a distance. If he was involved, however, it is likely that he had little to do with the overall design of the house, because in large part it was intended to closely resemble its predecessor. Instead, Mills may have been consulted about the house's overall fashionable appearance, but even that is not assured. It is clear from other projects with which Reiff and Hume were involved, that as part of a dispersal of a taste for Greek architecture the firm already was familiar with a suitable vocabulary. Beyond the capitals, much of the detailing they employed came from Benjamin's most recent treatise, *The Practical House Carpenter* (Boston, Author, 1830), wherein the author, who like his hero Bulfinch, seems to have undergone a stylistic conversion, presciently observed, "Since my last publication, the Roman school

---

[112] For the contract, see *Correspondence of Andrew Jackson*, ed. John S. Bassett (Washington, DC: Carnegie Institute of Washington, 1926–35), 5, 315–17, and for further references to the house and its rebuilding, 295–96, 298, 307–08, 343–44, 414. More generally, see James Patrick, *Architecture in Tennessee, 1789–1897* (Knoxville, TN: University of Tennessee Press, 1981), 171, 173, 176; and less reliably, Stanley F. Horn, *The Hermitage, Home of Old Hickory* (Richmond, VA: Garrett & Massie, 1938), 26–36.

[113] The connection with the Tower of the Winds was noted by Hamlin, *Greek Revival in America*, 238–39.

[114] Quoted from *Celebration of the Beginning of the American Patent System* (Washington, DC: Press of Gedney & Roberts, 1892), 465.

[115] From Jane B. Davies, "Six Letters by William P. Elliott to Alexander J. Davis, 1834–1838," *Journal of the Society of Architectural Historians* 26 (1967): 73. Since 1834 Elliot had been acting as an agent for Town and Davis in seeking federal commissions.

Figure 35. Architect unknown, possibly Robert Mills, The Hermitage, Davidson County, Tennessee.

HABS TENN, 19-NASH.V, 1-50; and HABS TENN, 19-NASH.V, 1-80.

of architecture has been entirely changed for the Grecian."[116] Despite his undefined role in its construction, Mills's interest in the Hermitage seems confirmed by his writing the president, August 3, 1836, when the rebuilding was complete, that he hoped Jackson "found your new mansion agreeable to your wishes," but at the same time this may simply have been a polite inquiry born of a genuine or self-serving friendship.[117]

As already noted, another who knew well and admired Latrobe and Bulfinch's work at the Capitol, was Alexander Jackson Davis. He had worked intermittently in Washington in 1830 and for several months in 1832 and 1833. Initially, he was sent there by Ithiel Town, with whom he had recently formed a partnership, in an attempt to secure for the firm Bulfinch's Office of Superintendent. Later he went to take careful drawings of the Capitol, of its façades, floor plans and interiors, the already cited drawing of the library included, in anticipation of issuing a portfolio of views, a project that never materialized, though several engravings and lithographs did result.[118] Davis, another committed Grecian, with reference to a volume borrowed from Town, marked his architectural beginnings in a diary entry for March 15, 1828: "First study of Stuart's Athens, from which I date Professional Practice."[119] It was directly from *The Antiquities of Athens* that his first expressed interest in the Tower of the Winds emerged. In a design for New York University, 1832, on the roof of a massive but highly restrained Doric façade Davis recreated the Tower (Figure 36), though with four entry porches all still with Doric details. With some knowledge of Wyatt's Radcliffe Observatory at Oxford, he possibly intended it for a similar academic purpose.[120] In any case his proposal was rejected, a Gothic design by Town and their recently admitted partner, James Dakin, being preferred for a collegiate structure.

---

[116] Asher Benjamin, *Practical House Carpenter, Being a Complete Development of the Grecian Orders of Architecture* (Boston: Author, 1830), iii. The volume, as its full title indicates, was given a pronounced Greek emphasis. Plate 28 serves as the source for the frontispiece of the Hermitage, but the Attic order finds no place amid the discussion of the orders. A second colonnade of six columns, accounted for in an additional estimate, August 23, 1836, with cast-iron Doric capitals was added on the rear of the house: see *Correspondence of Jackson*, 5, 414.

[117] Quoted from Liscombe, *Altogether American*, 185. Despite the lack of any evidence beyond the Elliot comments, Mills's level of involvement remains an issue. Liscombe, for example, has tried to attribute a drawing for the reconstruction to Mills, but the evidence offered is largely unconvincing: for the drawing and his views see *Altogether American*, 185–86. For assistance in trying to define Mills's role and answering related questions, I am indebted to Robbie Jones, Architectural Historian at the Hermitage.

[118] Undoubtedly, Davis even knew the building and its details earlier. As an apprentice typesetter, he had lived in Alexandria, 1818–23: see Jane B. Davies, "Alexander J. Davis, Creative American Architect," in *Alexander Jackson Davis, American Architect, 1803–1892*, ed. Amelia Peck (New York: Rizzoli for the Metropolitan Museum of Art, 1992), 25.

[119] Quoted from Davies, "Davis, Creative American Architect," 18.

[120] See Francis R. Kowsky, "Simplicity and Dignity: The Public and Institutional Building of Alexander Jackson Davis," in *Davis, American Architect*, ed. Peck, 49–50; and for another drawing, Paul Venable Turner, *Campus, An American Planning Tradition* (New York: Architectural History Foundation, 1984),. 122

— A Capital Problem —

Figure 36. Alexander Jackson Davis, design for New York University, 1832.
Collection of the New York Historical Society.

From his studies at the Capitol, Davis also found much to admire and bring to his own practice, most notably in his work at the North Carolina state house.[121] From the beginning of their partnership in 1829, he and Town had been active in the state, but their most important opportunity there came in 1833, when the firm was commissioned to rebuild the state house following the fire that had destroyed William Nichols's recently completed building. Previously, they had been unsuccessful in obtaining the reconstruction contract, it having been awarded to Nichols. Unlike Town and Davis, who proposed a Doric temple, much like their earlier designs for state houses in New Haven, Connecticut, 1827–1833, and Indianapolis, Indiana, 1831–1835, he prudently and successfully recommended a cruciform plan that approximated the appearance of his destroyed building.[122] However, because of the incompetence of

---

[121] As noted, for example, by Scott, *Temples*, 93.
[122] For Nichols' postfire design, see Peatross, *Nichols*, 12; and for Town and Davis and the North Carolina capitol, see Hitchcock and Seale, *Temples of Democracy*, 90–93; John L. Sanders, "The North Carolina State Capitol of 1840," *Antiques* 128 (1985): 474–83; Catherine W. Bishir, *North Carolina Architecture* (Chapel Hill, NC: University of North Carolina Press, 1990), 163–72; Lane, *Old South: Greek Revival and Romantic*, 59–65; and John L. Sanders, "Alexander Jackson Davis and the North Carolina State Capitol," in *A Romantic Architect in Antebellum North Carolina, The Works of Alexander Jackson Davis*, eds. Edward T Davis and John L. Sanders (Raleigh, NC: Historic Preservation Foundation of North Carolina, 2000), 36–56.

Figure 37. Alexander Jackson Davis, North Carolina State Capital, Raleigh, North Carolina, 1833–40. Exterior, Albert Barden Collection, North Carolina State Archives; and interior.

his son, who was delegated to supervise the work, Nichols soon was removed from the contract and Town and Davis were installed in his place. Although required to retain Nichols's already established foundations they did succeed in converting the east and west façades to elevated Doric tetrastyle porticos.[123]

With the Capitol in mind, the interiors too were given a distinctly Greek appearance. Providing for a bicameral legislature, the decision was made to model the state's House chamber on the federal House as reconfigured into an amphitheatre by Latrobe after 1815 and subsequently improved by Bulfinch. However, rather than using the Corinthian of the Choragic Monument that had been retained in the federal House chamber, Davis substituted the Attic that Latrobe had originally tried to impose on the hall (Figure 37). He employed it for the columns of the screen that flank the Speaker's desk and the curving colonnade at the rear.[124] However, his capitals do not precisely follow Latrobe's

---

[123] For these other state houses, see Kowsky, "Simplicity and Dignity," 40–44; and Hitchcock and Seale, *Temples of Democracy*, 76–93. Although the Connecticut project was begun by Town before Davis joined the firm, he was subsequently involved in its design.

[124] To sow a seed of doubt as regards responsibility for this detail and other aspects of the interior, despite the Town and Davis drawing, the question remains as to how much of the design and ornamentation originally may have been by William Nichols?

variant on the order with their stems and flowers between the waterleaves, but like those employed in the South Carolina Library, Davis imitated the plainer Athenian originals. Additionally, recalling perhaps Latrobe's House vestibule and staircase at the Capitol, in the State House the east and west wing entry halls and their adjoining stairwells have the Ionic on the ground floor, the same Ionic that decorates the state's Senate chamber, whereas the upper level replicates the Attic style of the House.

As observed thus far the usage of the Attic order in America does have a distinct genealogy. Although there certainly are examples of its application that fall outside these lines of descent, notably by the early Bulfinch at the Massachusetts State House, in its initial ascendancy it is largely the work of acknowledged architects and it works its way from Latrobe to Bulfinch at the Capitol and then in the 1830s to Mills and Davis. Following after them, the next generation to use the Attic includes the brothers James and Charles Dakin; James Gallier, a learned architect who arrived from England in 1832; and Minard Lefever, all of whom interconnect with each other and with Davis. The Dakins and Gallier all passed through the New York offices of Town and Davis, and subsequently James Dakin and Gallier were both involved with Lafever. In 1829 James Dakin, having completed his apprenticeship with Town and Davis, had become an associate of the firm and, as noted above, a partner from May 1832 to November 1833, just when they were beginning work on the Raleigh State House. On resigning he did some drafting for Lafever and briefly practiced on his own before sailing to New Orleans in 1835. Gallier, after arriving in New York, worked for several months at Town and Davis where Charles Dakin had also found employment. On leaving Town and Davis, Gallier briefly worked for James Dakin and was in a short-term partnership with Minard Lefever.[125] In 1834 in company with Charles Dakin he sailed south to New Orleans where the pair formed the firm of Gallier and Dakin, only to dissolve it the following year when, with the arrival of James Dakin, Dakin and Dakin was created. Even Town and Davis was a short-lived partnership, being dissolved in 1835 when Davis departed the firm. If anything, this somewhat complex account of relationships does demonstrate the dynamics and identifies the leading personalities by which Greek Revival architecture increasingly made its way to the Deep South, to places where the various projects of William Nichols already were preparing receptive and sympathetic audiences for this new style.

---

[125] For James Dakin and Lefever, see Jacob Landy, *The Architecture of Minard Lafever* (New York: Columbia University Press, 1970), 45, and for both Dakins in his office, Arthur Scully Jr., *James Dakin, Architect, His Career in New York and the South* (Baton Rouge, LA: Louisiana State University Press, 1973), 38–9.

10

American Variants on the Attic Order

— A Capital Problem —

Recalling the Adam brothers' earlier departures it was just about this time and emanating from this group that decorative and more fulsome American variants on the Attic became available and achieved a rapid acceptance and dispersal. The invention of Minard Lefever (Figure 38), these new capitals were included in his *Beauties of Modern Architecture* (New York, 1835), a volume for which both Gallier and Charles Dakin had drawn plates when in his employ.[126] For the key design, his plate 11, Lefever retained the capital's roundness, added a third register of leaves at the bottom, and introduced flowers between the acanthus leaves at the middle. Finally, at the top, the wholly abstracted waterleaves bend over and curl outward, exposing an upper edge of decorative gadrooning.[127] For gallery fronts or as part of a system of sliding doors a reduced version was introduced, Lafever's plates X and Y, where the gadrooning is retained, but the references to nature in the leaves were removed in favor of abstract fluted motifs (Figure 39).[128] Both renditions quickly came into use, initially in the architecture of Gallier and the Dakins.

Once settled in New Orleans, Gallier and Charles Dakin found quick success in their practice. An early commission to the firm, December 1834, was from three New Orleans gentlemen for three adjoining town houses, which the owners came to call the "Three Sisters."[129] Frame two-story structures, their porticoed and pedimented façades were each supported by four giant columns (Figure 40) that clearly derive from Lefever's plate 11. Even prior to arriving in New Orleans, during a brief stopover in Mobile, Alabama, Gallier and Dakin picked up a prestigious commission, Government Street Presbyterian Church, on whose design they continued to work even after their departure from the city.[130] Recalling on its formidable exterior the distyle in antis popularized by Town and Davis, the interior is remarkably light and open. The reredos, with its battered walls, has an Egyptian flavor, but is supported by four Corinthian columns. The galleries, however, rest on a series

---

[126] Although he did not include their Attic capital, several of Lafever's other plates are derived from the *Antiquities of Athens*, for which see Landy, *Lafever*, 29–30, 252 n. 3. For the contribution of Dakin and Gallier to *Beauties* and by Gallier to an earlier volume, *The Modern Builder's Guide* (New York: Henry C. Sleight, Collins & Hannay, 1833), see Landy, *Lafever*, 49. For the variants on the capital also see Clay Lancaster, *Antebellum Architecture of Kentucky* (Lexington, KY: University Press of Kentucky, 1991), 189.

[127] The accompanying remarks, which include no specific references as to the order's Greek origin, do observe: "This is a design composed of antique specimens, and reduced to accurate proportions; with a view to render it acceptable in many places; instead of the standard orders."

[128] For the sliding doors, see plate 7 whose accompanying remarks noted, "Plate 11 is the base column and capital on an enlarged scale, adapted to practical purposes."

[129] The houses were torn down c. 1950. For them, see *The Autobiography of James Gallier, Architect* (Paris, 1864; reprinted New York: De Capo Press, 1973), 33–34; and Scully, *Dakin*, 40.

[130] For the church see Scully, *Dakin*, 68–72; *Autobiography of Gallier*, 21; and Elizabeth Barrett Gould, *From Port to Port, An Architectural History of Mobile Alabama, 1711–1918* (Tuscaloosa, AL: University of Alabama Press, 1988), 66–68.

Figure 38. Minard Lefever, *Beauties of Modern Architecture* (New York: D. Appleton & Co., 1835), pl. 11.A.

Figure 39. Minard Lefever, *Beauties of Modern Architecture* (New York: D. Appleton & Co., 1835).

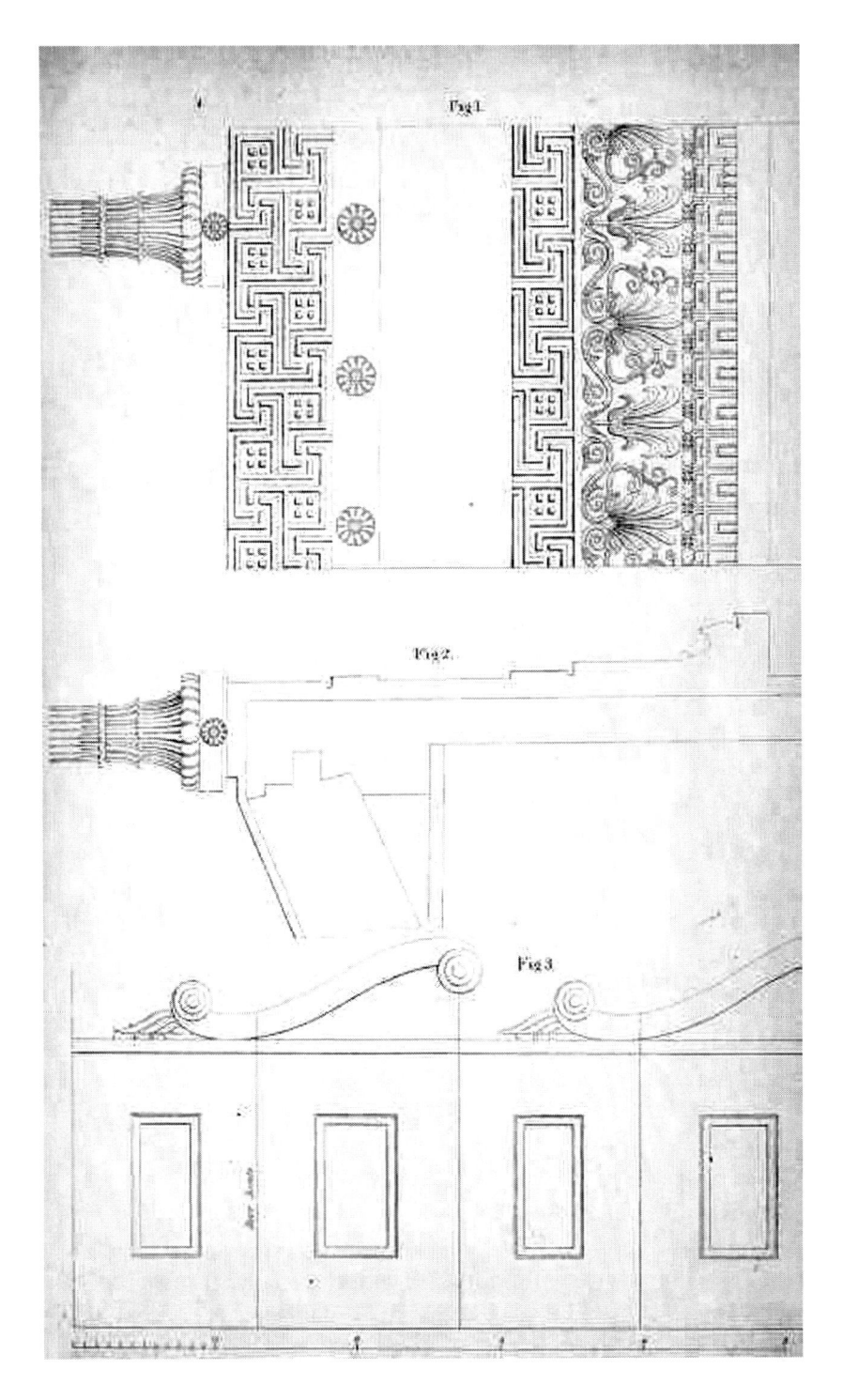

Figure 40. James Gallier and Charles Dakin, The Three Sisters, New Orleans, Louisiana, c. 1835.

New Orleans Public Library; and detail, HABS No. La-1441.

of columns whose capitals follow Lafever's plate 48 (Figure 41).[131] Built in 1836–37, construction persisted through the breakup of Gallier and Dakin and the formation of Dakin and Dakin, with the result that assigning specific details remains difficult, especially in this instance where both Gallier and James Dakin had worked in Lefever's office.[132]

---

[131] Scully, *Dakin*, 72, notes Charles Dakin's copy of Lafever's *Beauties*, with the notation "Charles B. Dakin, Mobile, Ala."

[132] On this confusion, see Scully, *Dakin*, 71.

— A Capital Problem —

Figure 41. James Gallier and Charles Dakin, Government Street Presbyterian Church, Mobile, Alabama, 1836–37.

Interior, HABS ALA, 49-MOBI, 1-7.

With the growing dominance of the Greek Revival style in the succeeding years, at least through 1860, the use of the Attic order in its various forms can be observed to have proliferated. However, although it obtained a broad geographic distribution and a wide a variety of applications, being used in both public and domestic buildings, it must be observed that it never succeeded in equaling or supplanting the canonical three. Always, the Doric, Ionic, and Corinthian orders predominated, but the Attic did provide occasional relief from these established orders by offering an opportunity to introduce variety while maintaining Grecian authenticity. The means of its transmission are diverse and potentially complex, for in application it could just as well be found in the designs of an established architect as in the construction of a master or lesser builder or carpenter. It could be modeled after an actual example or imitate a detailed engraving in a widely distributed architectural handbook. Besides the actual examples provided by Latrobe and his followers and admirers, Stuart and Revett's *Antiquities of Athens*, both in its original edition and in reprints, London, 1825 and 1837, remained an important architectural text, but, as already cited, the Attic also could be conveniently found in Benjamin's *American Builder's Companion*, a volume directly addressed to the American craftsman.[133] Alternatively, there was Lafever's plate 11 from his similarly directed *Beauties*, though he provided no indication of its ancient source or made any claim for its antique legitimacy. Instead, through his transformation the capital became part of a larger revivalist vocabulary, one option among several that might be used in obtaining a certain architectural appearance. Attesting to their satisfying a particular need in the dispersal of a style, the *Builder's Companion* and the *Beauties of Modern Architecture* went through several editions and had a remarkably widespread circulation, significantly influencing generations of rural carpenters and builders.[134]

Certainly Lafever's version quickly gained ascendancy in both private and public architecture. Just as the Attic had obtained an American legitimacy it too obtained a national validation and came to be used on buildings erected by the federal government outside Washington and by various state and municipal authorities. For the Boston customhouse authorized by Congress in 1835 and built between 1837 and 1847, the New England architect Ammi Burnham Young won a competition with a domed Grecian design that used an Athenian Doric on the exterior, but for the twelve attached columns encircling the

---

[133] See Daniel D. Reiff, *Houses from Books: Treatises, Pattern Books, and Catalogs in American Architecture, 1738–1950* (University Park, PA: Pennsylvania State University Press, 2000), esp. 16–45. The 1832 reprint of the *Antiquities of Athens* included a fifth volume edited by Cockerell.

[134] See Damie Stillman, "Architectural Books in New York: From McComb to Lafever," in Hafertepe and O'Gorman, *American Architects*, 172–74. For handbooks also see the discussion in Harris, *Architectural Books*, 38–40.

— A Capital Problem —

Figure 42. John S. Norris, United States Custom House, Savannah, Georgia, 1848–52. Exterior photo by Sarah O.; and detail, General Services Administration.

interior rotunda Lafever's plate 11 was preferred.[135] John Norris, a New Yorker who developed an extensive southern practice, also used the Attic on his federal customs houses in Wilmington, North Carolina, 1843–47, where it capped a pair of attached columns in a temple front, and subsequently in Savannah (Figure 42), where it served as part of a hexastyle pediment portico, 1848–52.[136] In writing of Norris's buildings, the respective local newspapers noted the use of the Attic with a specificity that suggests knowledgeable writers and readers, the former informed perhaps by the architect. To quote The *Wilmington*

---

[135] See Lawrence Wodehouse, "Architectural Projects in the Greek Revival Style by Ammi Burnham Young," *Old–Time New England* 60 (1970): 73–74, 77, 80; and Daniel M. Bluestone, "City and Aesthetic Reserve: Ammi Burnham Young's 1850s Federal Customhouse Designs," *Winterthur Annual* 25 (1990): 273–74.

[136] See Lee, *Architects to the Nation*, 22–23; and Mary Lane Morrison, *John S. Norris, Architect in Savannah, 1846–1860* (Savannah, GA: Beehive Press, 1980), 6–23. At the same time Norris designed a Savannah town house for Andrew Low, 1849, which included a front door and interior pilasters complete with Lafever's Attic capitals, for which see Morrison, *Norris*, 43; and Lane, *Old South: Greek Revival and Romantic*, 113–15.

Journal, the columns were "after the manner of the Temple of the Winds at Athens."[137]

At the state level the most important public project to use Lafevre's version was yet another Alabama state house, erected this time in Montgomery following the city's selection in 1846 as the state's permanent capital in place of Tuscaloosa. Following a competition the commission was awarded to Stephen Decatur Button, another New York architect who worked in the south, albeit briefly before returning north and settling in Philadelphia. However, as a surviving drawing of the front façade indicates (Figure 43), rather than burying the historical Attic order on the interior, the winning design used a familiar variant on the exterior. Its monumental hexastyle portico, as a local journalist noted, was composed of "columns of the Grecian composite style of architecture. The design was taken from Lafever's *Beauties of Modern Architecture*."[138] Built in 1846–47, it stood until 1849 when it was destroyed by fire, only to be rebuilt, 1850–51, by Daniel Pratt. A New England builder and architect trained in the Greek Revival, Pratt first worked in Georgia. After inventing an improved cotton gin he moved to Alabama where he became a prominent industrialist, but continued to practice his original profession. Erected along very similar lines as its predecessor, Pratt's capitol retained a hexastyle portico and as before the supporting columns were capped by capitals after Lafever (Figure 44).[139]

Descending within this hierarchical governmental structure it was within patronage at county level that the Attic as a classical order had its most widespread application, initially in revivalist temple-fronted buildings that seem to derive from Mill's work in South Carolina or later as with so many other

---

[137] For the newspaper accounts, see Morrison, *Norris*, 56–58; and Lane, *Old South: Greek Revival and Romantic*, 111–12. At Savannah, Norris's design was anticipated by that of the unsuccessful custom house submission of Charles B. Cluskey. Irish born like Gallier, Cluskey arrived in New York in 1829, and subsequently had several periods of residence in Savannah, where he first used the Attic on the Aaron Champion house, 1842, and the Henry McAlpin house (The Hermitage), c. 1845, before including it on the two porticos of his unsuccessful customs house design, 1846 or early 1847; for the architect and these various commissions, see Lane, *Old South: Greek Revival and Romantic*, 103, 106–07. In Wilmington, eventually demolished in 1915, the Norris customs house was replaced by a federal office building and courthouse designed by James A. Wetmore, 1916–19, that extensively used attached columns with the Attic order. Norris also designed a customs house with Attic columns in Wheeling, West Virginia, 1856–60; Lee, *Architects to the Nation*, 62.

[138] Quoted from an extensive description in the *Daily Alabama Journal*, March 12, 1850, and attributed to Button by Lane, *Old South: Greek Revival and Romantic*, 115–18, who also reproduces the drawing. For further on the building, with its cast-iron capitals, see Hitchcock and Seale, *Temples of Democracy*, 125–26.

[139] For Pratt's career and his capitol, see Robert L. Raley, "Daniel Pratt, Architect and Builder in Georgia," *Antiques*, 102 (1972): 425–32; Donna C. Hole, "Daniel Pratt and Barachias Holt: Architect of the Alabama State Capitol?," *The Alabama Review* 37 (1084): 83–97, who raises the question of responsibility since Pratt died in 1850; and Robert Gamble, *The Alabama Catalog*, rev. ed. (Tuscaloosa, AL: University of Alabama Press, 1987), 6–7, 193–94, 323–34.

— A Capital Problem —

Figure 43. Stephen D. Button, design for Alabama State Capitol, Montgomery, Alabama, built 1846–47, destroyed by fire 1849.

Alabama Department of Archives and History, Montgomery, AL.

building types done in a variety of styles, as an ornamental detail.[140] An early example of the former is the Chenango County courthouse in Norwich, New York. Authorized by the state legislature in 1837, its designer remains unknown. Indicative of the sort of confusion that continues to surround this unfamiliar order, an early description noted that it had a "portico supported upon four Corinthian columns."[141] A better known example is in Petersburg, Virginia, 1838–40, where Calvin Pollard, yet another New York practitioner working in the South, used the Athenian Attic on the portico and tower of the local

---

[140] For a discussion of the movement of the classical style from the federal level to the local, and for illustrations of many temple-fronted courthouses, see Henry-Russell Hitchcock and William Seale, "Notes on the Architecture," in *Court House: A Photographic Documentation*, ed. Richard Pare (New York: Horizon Press, 1978), 165, 171, 172–85, who see Washington architecture and Jefferson's Virginia state capitol as major precedents..

[141] The quote from an unidentified source is cited in Herbert Alan Johnson and Ralph K. Andrist, *Historic Courthouses of New York State: 18th and 19th Century Halls of Justice Across the Empire State* (New York: Columbia University Press, 1977), 32–33. For a later New York example, the Oswego County courthouse in Pulaski, authorized in 1858 and constructed 1859–60 to the design of Zina D. Stephens, a local architect, see 122–25.

Figure 44. Daniel Pratt, Alabama State Capitol, Montgomery, Alabama, as rebuilt 1850–51. Photo by J. Michael Dockery.

courthouse.[142] In Massachusetts, Ammi B. Young, having already introduced the Attic on the federal custom house, would continue his use of the order at the county level. In Worcester, for the eponymous county, from 1843 to 1845 he undertook a courthouse whose façade was marked by a colonnade comprised of six monumental granite columns.[143] By contrast, recalling their uses on the Tower of the Winds, in 1848 when renovating Bulfinch's 1814–16 Middlesex county courthouse in Cambridge, Massachusetts, Young installed six lesser Attic columns to support a single-story porch that ran across the façade.[144] And well into midcentury, just as the Attic continued to be used, appearing, for example, in a cast-iron version on the 1867–68 temple-fronted Moniteau county courthouse in California, Missouri, whose design may be due to its superintendent of building, William Vogdt.[145] Likewise, Lafevre's plate 11, as an American order, also had its partisans, for example, the unknown designer of the 1854 Montgomery County, Alabama, courthouse, though for this detail Pratt's nearby state house might have served as a stimulus.[146]

Dropping down still further, to service at the municipal level, recalling the role of the Tower of the Winds as an observatory, in 1841, there was the aforementioned 1841 New Orleans fire station, The Louisiana Hose Company, where James Dakin incorporated a variant on the Tower as a roof structure, also ornamented with Lafever's order.[147]

Among public buildings, the order's rarest appearance was in churches and here too Lafever's design was preferred. Until the Gothic Revival came to dominate in midnineteenth century, churches tended to follow the English classical style largely established by Christopher Wren and James Gibbs, which featured temple fronts adorned with Roman details. Promptly imported into the American colonies after the nation's establishment, the use of Greek elements on these façades eventually came to dominate, perhaps in an attempt to disassociate the variety of Christian denominations from the Roman church

---

[142] See John O. Peters and Margaret T. Peters, *Virginia's Historic Courthouses* (Charlottesville, VA: University Press of Virginia, 1995), 114–116, who note that the tower was not part of the original plan, but was authorized during construction; also Pare, *Court House*, 176. For Pollard's classicism, see Stillman, "Architectural Books in New York," 170–72; and generally for the Grecianism of New York architects during this period, Landy, *Lafever*, 47–53: and for their working in the South, Lane, *Old South: Greek Revival and Romantic*, 98–125.

[143] Pare, *Court House*, 177–78.

[144] For the building and the renovations, see Kirker, *Bulfinch*, 295–97; Lawrence Wodehouse, "Ammi Burnham Young, 1798–1874," *Journal of the Society of Architectural Historians* 25 (1966), 273–74; and Susan E. Maycock, *East Cambridge*, rev. ed. (Cambridge, MA: MA MIT Press for Cambridge Historical Commission, 1988), 131–37.

[145] See "Historic Missouri Courthouses: Moniteau County Courthouse," *Missouri Historical Review* 58.1 (October, 1963): inside cover; and Pare, *Court House*, pl. 67. The use of cast iron suggests that the capital in this form must have been somewhat widely available as a catalogue item from some foundry.

[146] See Gamble, *Alabama Catalog*, 70, 75. For the use of still other variants, see Pare, *Court House*, pls. 56 (South Bend, Indiana, by John Mills Van Osdel; 1855) and 61 (Colusa, California; 1861).

[147] Scully, *Dakin*, 103–04.

while still maintaining a familiar and fashionable appearance.[148] Yet unlike Britain, where, as already noticed in the work of Soane and the Inwoods, various architects occasionally included the Attic on their exterior and interior ecclesiastical designs, in America the order seems to have been confined to church interiors and then to Lafever's variant. Government Street Presbyterian church with its galleries taken directly from his *Beauties of Modern Architecture* already had been introduced, but largely on the basis of their use of details taken from his publications, two churches are also attributed directly to Lafever himself; St. James, an 1835–37 Catholic church in lower Manhattan repeats plate 48 for its galleries, as does the Whaler's Church at Sag Harbor, 1843–44.[149] Beyond these examples, significant uses of plate 11 have been identified in the First Parish Church, 1840, in Duxbury, Massachusetts, a prosperous shipbuilding community, where a pair of massive columns, undoubtedly carefully crafted by a local carpenter, support the choir loft, and also, contrasting with its pedimented Doric temple facade, on the interior of Thomas Ustick Walter's Tabb Street Presbyterian Church, 1843, in Petersburg, Virginia (Figure 45).[150] Of the Stuart and Revett Attic in a church, no example has yet presented itself in nineteenth-century America.

---

[148] See Hamlin, *Greek Revival in America*, 344–45 and passim.
[149] For these churches, see Landy, *Lafever*, 217–34. With its otherwise Egyptian Revival exterior, Sag Harbor may descend from an earlier scheme by Alexander Jackson Davis.
[150] See Alexandra B. Earle, "History in Towns: Duxbury, Massachusetts," *Antiques* 131 (1987): 621–23; and for the Walter church, Kennedy, *Greek Revival America*, 376.

— A Capital Problem —

Figure 45. Thomas Ustick Walter, Tabb Street Presbyterian Church, Petersburg, Virginia, 1843.

Interior, HABS VA, 27-PET, 30-6.

11

The Attic Order, Its Variants, and American Domestic Architecture

— A Capital Problem —

In domestic architecture the situation was entirely different. The proliferation of publications in recent years that focus on state and local architecture confirms the dispersal of Greek Revival architecture prior to the Civil War in the northern, southern, and western states, including the use of Attic capitals and, in fewer instances, Lafever's invention, plate 11. Peaking in the 1840s and in the South, these details, though in far fewer appearances than the canonical three, could be found on a wide range of housing, from mansions of prodigious size to more modest dwellings and in rural, town, or city settings.[151] Whether encouraged by a desire to be fashionable and contemporary or intended as some sort of nationalistic expression, the Attic as part of a rising new taste was most prominently displayed on exteriors, though in some instances it served as a lesser decorative element on the interior. Moreover, in general the dispersal and usage of such Greek motifs also marked the shift from designs originating with architects who conceived of a house as a stylistic whole and commonly consulted archaeological and learned tomes, to those provided by provincial builders and carpenters, craftsmen who derived their details from conveniently available handbooks like Lafever's or Benjamin's and applied them to vernacular construction.[152]

Prominent examples of monumental façades incorporating columns topped by Attic capitals include the Gordon Hewitt house, 1833, and several other homes from the next decade in the same classical revival town of Owego, New York; in Pittsburgh, Pennsylvania, c. 1835, the William Croghan residence; the Peter Augustus Jay Mansion, built on the site of his father, John Jay's house, Rye, New York, 1838 (Figure 46); the Hoxey house, 1840s, in Columbus, Georgia; and the Kerrison house, c. 1842 in Charleston, South Carolina, a design sometimes attributed to Russell Warren.[153] In Montgomery, Alabama, the William Knox, c. 1848, and Perly Gerald, c. 1858, houses have similar façades, as do Richard Ludlum's home, c. 1848, in Richmond, Virginia; and in Maury County, Tennessee, not far from Jackson's Hermitage, Manor Hall,

---

[151] With regard to its more frequent occurrence in the South, it has been noted that the precedent of antiquity not only lingered but was reinforced there in the decades immediately preceding the Civil War, for the past offered the presumed model of a great civilization coexisting with slavery often in small independent nation states, for which, see Edwin A. Miles, "The Young American Nation and the Classical World," *Journal of the History of Ideas* 35 (1974): 268–69, 273–74.

[152] On these points see Dell Upton, "Pattern Books and Professionalism: Aspects of the Transformation of Domestic Architecture in America, 1800–1860," *Winterthur Portfolio* 19 (summer/autumn 1984): 118–20, 128–30, 149–50..

[153] For these residences, see variously: Joan Buchman, "Owego Architecture: The Greek Revival in a Pioneer Town," *Journal, Society of Architectural Historians* 25 (1966): 220; Charles M. Stotz, *The Early Architecture of Western Pennsylvania*, new ed. (Pittsburgh, PA: University of Pittsburgh Press, 1995), 128, 131; Kenneth Severns, *Charleston Antebellum Architecture and Civic Destiny* (Knoxville, TN: University of Tennessee Press, 1988), 123–24, and for the attribution of the Kerrison House to Warren, Jonathan H. Poston, *The Buildings of Charleston: A Guide to the City's Architecture* (Charleston, SC: University Of South Carolina Press, 1997) 576–77, and Beatrice St. Julien Ravenel, *The Architects of Charleston* (Charleston, SC: Carolina Art Association,1945), 149–6; Gamble, *Historical Architecture in Alabama*, 69, 74.

Figure 46. Architect unknown, Peter Augustus Jay House, Rye, New York, 1838.

— A Capital Problem —

c. 1849, and the Nathaniel Cheairs house, c. 1855, also known as Rippaville.[154] Still on the same scale but using Lafever's version, there are the Shepherd house, c. 1840, attributed to Russell Warren in Providence, Rhode Island; Frances Costigan's Lanier house, 1840–44, in another classical revival town, Madison, Indiana; the Salem Copeland house, 1847, in Worcester, Massachusetts; Pembroke Hall, 1840s, at Edenton, North Carolina; and Stanton Hall, 1857–58, in Natchez, Mississippi.[155] Recalling the presence of the Dakin brothers and Gallier in New Orleans, that city too saw several uses of the Attic and its variant, notably on the Jacob U. Payne house, c. 1842–50; and in the 1850s on several houses in the Garden District.[156] Chicago too has an example in the Charles J. Hull House, 1856, by an unknown architect, which eventually served as the first home of Jane Addams's Hull House Settlement.[157]

Used in a lesser dimension and sometimes recalling the original Tower of the Winds portico, several homes are known which include entry porches and doorways that use Attic capitals, such as the portico added in 1830 to the Virginia Governor's mansion in Richmond, an 1814 Federalist house designed originally by Alexander Parris, and still used in the 1830s in several Princeton, New Jersey, dwellings by a local Greek enthusiast, Charles Steadman.[158] Other examples are on the Dr. Daniel Edgar Fisher house, c. 1840, at Edgartown, Martha's Vineyard; the Avery Downer house, 1842, in Granville, Ohio; for a secondary porch on Rattle and Snap, c. 1845, at Columbia, Tennessee; and

---

[154] D. Gregory Jeane, ed., *The Architectural Legacy of the Lower Chattahoochee Valley in Alabama and Georgia* (Tuscaloosa, AL: Published for the Historic Chattahoochee Commission by the University of Alabama Press, 1978), 74–76; Lane, *Old South: Greek Revival and Romantic*, 156; and Patrick, *Architecture in Tennessee*, 153, 174, 177, 181, 195.

[155] For these houses, see Antoinette F. Downing, *Early Houses of Rhode Island* (Richmond, VA: Garrett and Massie, 1937), 445, 457; John T. Windle, *The Early Architecture of Madison Indiana* (Madison, IN: Historic Madison, 1986), 78–81, 87–88; Stanley Schuler, *New England Homes* rev. ed. (Atglen, PA: Schiffer Publishing, 2000), 182–83; Lane, *Old South: Greek Revival and Romantic*, 161; Mary W. Crocker, *Historical Architecture in Mississippi* (Jackson, MS: University and College Press of Mississippi, 1973), 38–41. Other examples include the Savannah houses by Cluskey, for which, see note 132 supra.

[156] See Joan G. Caldwell, "Urban Growth, 1815–1860: Diverse Tastes—Greek, Gothic and Italianate," in *Louisiana Buildings*, eds. Jessie Poesch and Barbara SoRelle Bacot (Baton Rouge, LA: Louisiana State University Press, 1997), 193–94; and Friends of the Cabildo, *New Orleans Architecture, 1, The Lower Garden District* (Gretna, LA: Friends of the Cabildo and Pelican Publishing, 1971), 70, 97, 120.

[157] Franz Schultz and Kevin Harrington, *Chicago's Famous Buildings*, 5th ed. (Chicago: University of Chicago Press, 2003), 212–13.

[158] See William Seale, *Virginia's Executive Mansion: A History of the Governor's House* (Richmond, VA: Published for the Citizens Advisory Council for Interpreting and Furnishing the Executive Mansion by the Virginia State Library and Archives, 1988), 20–30; Reiff, *Houses from Books*, 42–45; Constance M. Greiff, Mary W. Gibbons, and Elizabeth G.C. Menzies, *Princeton Architecture, A Pictorial History of Town and Campus* (Princeton, NJ: Princeton University Press, 1967): 90–94; and Robert P. Guter and Janet W. Foster, *Building by the Book: Pattern Book Architecture in New Jersey* (New Brunswick, NJ: Rutgers University Press, 1992), 42–45.

in 1840s Owego, on the Hollenbeck house.[159] In Madison, Indiana, c. 1848, Costigan used the order for his own modest townhouse.[160] Again other builders preferred Lafever's version and in 1845 it is found in Lexington, Kentucky on the doorway to the Philip Swigert House and in Owego during the same decade on the Downs and Odell Gregory homes.[161] And there are several known uses on interiors, including Sturdivant Hall, c. 1845, in Selma, Alabama; for the dining room pilasters of General Leavenworth's house, 1845, in Syracuse New York; and again on the entrance hall to Rattle and Snap.[162] The Attic also appears in the mistress's bedroom of one of the last of the great antebellum mansions, Gaineswood in Demopolis, Alabama, 1842–60, designed and built by Gen. Nathaniel B. Whitfield.[163] Needless to say there are still other examples of these varied uses of the Attic that have been overlooked in this brief litany, not to speak of those instances of which all trace has been lost, but for housing this surviving evidence does demonstrate the geographic and chronological range within which the order had a regular, even ubiquitous, appearance.

---

[159] See Wendell Garrett, *Classic America: The Federal Style and Beyond* (New York: Rizzoli, 1992), 59; Richard N. Campen, *Ohio, An Architectural Portrait* (Chagrin Falls, OH: West Summit Press, 1973), 67–69; Patrick, *Architecture in Tennessee*, 153–54, 170–71, 179, 181; Alexander B. Trowbridge, "The Greek Revival in Owego and Near-by New York Towns," *The White Pine Series* 7, no. 3 (1921): 9, 14, 16; and Buchman, "Owego Architecture," 218, 220.

[160] Windle, *Madison Indiana*, 78–81, 87–88.

[161] See Lancaster, *Kentucky*, 189–90; and Alexander B. Trowbridge, "The Greek Revival in Owego and Nearby New York Towns," *The White Pine Series* 7, no, 3 (1921): 2–16.

[162] See Architects' Emergency Committee, *Great Georgian Houses of America* (New York: Kalkhoff Press, 1933–37), 2, 165–70; and Mills Lane, *Architecture of the Old South: Kentucky and Tennessee* (Savannah, GA: Beehive Foundation, 1993), 179–80. Another example is the Norris' Low House, 1850, for which, see note 132 supra.

[163] Gamble, *Historical Architecture in Alabama*, 76–77, 275–76.

12

The Attic Order in Decline

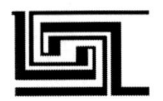

— A Capital Problem —

Bringing this survey to a close there were two notable uses of the Attic capital at midcentury, when the energies of the Greek Revival in America already were dissipating, that appropriately reflect back on several of the major issues and personalities considered previously, notably to Jefferson and Latrobe whose conflicting tastes were central to the order's introduction and fate. Involved were Robert Mills in 1852 at the University of Virginia at Charlottesville and Thomas Ustick Walter in 1855 at the Capitol. Mills already has been identified as a student of Latrobe and a committed Grecian. Walter, who was of the next generation, had studied under Strickland, Mill's contemporary in Latrobe's studio, and shared their common architectural taste.[164] But in these two commissions both men, like Latrobe before them, come up against the Roman bias of Thomas Jefferson, whether as the genius responsible for the University of Virginia or as the man so much behind the initial designs of the Capitol. And on both these projects Latrobe also had a visible presence, for besides his work on the Capitol, during the summer of 1817, several months prior to his resignation from his second term as Surveyor of the City of Washington and Superintendent of its Buildings, he also had assisted Jefferson with designs for the newly founded university.[165]

Regardless of their contrasting, even conflicting, tastes there always had been a sufficiently strong affinity between Latrobe and Jefferson to encourage a mutual admiration, even dependency, when it came to matters architectural. Although yielding somewhat to Latrobe's persistence, Jefferson had finally permitted the intrusion of some Greek orders in the Capitol, none were to be included on the ten pavilions that initially constituted his "Academical village," several of which Latrobe designed. In the variety of their appearances, as he informed Latrobe in June 1817, Jefferson intended that they would "serve as specimens of orders for the architectural lectures." Included were Doric, Ionic, and Corinthian examples, all taken from another Romanist handbook Fréart de Chambray's *Parallèle d'Architecture*.[166] There was no space for any distinctly Grecian versions, much less the Attic.[167] Nor did the authentically Greek orders find any place on the centerpiece of Jefferson's campus,

---

[164] For this "line of descent," see the remarks of Latrobe's son John H.B. Latrobe, *The Capitol and Washington at the Beginning of the Present Century* (Baltimore: William K. Boyle, 1881), 29–30.

[165] See Hamlin, *Latrobe*, 468–70; Patricia C. Sherwood and Joseph Michael Lasala "Education and Architecture: The Evolution of the University of Virginia's Academical Village," in *Thomas Jefferson's Academical Village, The Creation of an Architectural Masterpiece*, ed. Richard Guy Wilson (Charlottesville, VA: Bayly Art Museum of the University of Virginia, 1973), 17–33.

[166] BHL to Jefferson, June 17, 1817: Van Horne and Formwalt, *Correspondence of Latrobe*, 3, 901–02. For Latrobe's work at the University, see Fiske Kimball, *Thomas Jefferson, Architect* (Boston: Riverside Press, 1916), 186–92, 200–05; and for the Palladianism, William B. O'Neal, *Jefferson's Buildings at the University of Virginia* (Charlottesville, VA: University of Virginia Press, 1960).

[167] The identity and source of each order is annotated on a copy of Peter Maverick's c. 1822 engraving of the University, for which see Kimball, *Jefferson, Architect*, after pl. 233. Also see BHL to Jefferson, October 12, 1817: Van Horne and Formwalt, *Correspondence of Latrobe*, 3955.

the Rotunda, the classroom and library building he designed as a Palladian rendition of the Roman Pantheon. In July 1817, accompanying a campus plan that included a building very much like the Pantheon, Latrobe had recommended a "Center building which ought to exhibit in Mass and details as perfect a specimen of good Architectural taste as can be devised."[168] Begun in 1823, well after Latrobe's death, the Rotunda was completed three years later, shortly after his own death. At the north end, looking outward over the lawn and the pavilions and colonnades that frame it on the east and west, the Rotunda's front, its south façade, was marked like the Pantheon by a hexastyle Corinthian portico.

By the early 1850s, the university's trustees realized that the Rotunda was no longer adequate for the institution's needs. Additional space was required and the commission for an extension, the Annex as it was dubbed, went to Robert Mills, who noted,

> The great increase of students in the University and the want of suitable rooms for their exercises have caused the erection of a building in the rear of the Rotunda, 150 feet long including Porticoes, and 50 feet wide, which from the declivity of the ground, will afford 4 large lecture rooms, a large exhibition room and museum above, all accessible from the Rotunda, from which it is separated by a colonnaded space.[169]

The Trustees may have selected Mills because of his prominence and reputation as a designer in the classical mode, but doubtless also affecting their decision was a recollection of his personal connection to Jefferson, whom he met around 1801 and with whom he remained in touch until the president's death. It was under Jefferson's guidance that he developed his knowledge of Roman architecture, sufficient that by 1803 he was assisting with the design of Monticello.[170] A few years later, under Latrobe's tutelage, he converted. Indirectly, he would recall this change in some remarks of May 1, 1850, which were included in his futile attempt to obtain the commission to extend the Capitol, the same commission that went to Walter. Though their salutary tone may have had an expeditious ring, marking him for the position as Latrobe's most suitable heir, his laudatory respectfulness nevertheless should not be distrusted. As he said, "the *whole*

---

[168] Van Horne and Formwalt, *Correspondence of Latrobe*, 3, 914–16; and for additional correspondence between the two related to the university, 899–910. For the plan and building, also see William B. O'Neal, *Jefferson's Buildings at the University of Virginia, The Rotunda* (Charlottesville, VA: 1960).

[169] Robert Mills, "Architecture in Virginia," *The Virginia Historical Register and Literary Companion* 6 (1853): 41.

[170] Earlier he also worked under Hoban and Thornton. For these early professional associations as well as that with Jefferson, see Bryan, *America's First Architect*, 10–22; and Kimball, *Jefferson, Architect*, 68, 71, 165–66.

Union is indebted to Mr. Latrobe for introducing a *correct* taste in architecture into our country at a time when but little was known here of the art."[171]

The Annex's "Northern Front," Mills wrote, "is ornamented by a similar Portico to that of the Rotunda, in which will be placed the Statue of Mr. Jefferson."[172] However, rather than having a pediment above, this façade was marked by a flat entablature carried as before on colossal Corinthian columns. The shafts were to be of stone, but recalling the difficulties of several earlier efforts to obtain well-carved capitals, it was decided to have them cast in iron by a Richmond foundry, Samson & Pae. Their cost proposal sent to Mills on April 9, 1852, was for the furnishing of the "Capitals for the Columns & pilasters for the Portico and interior of the Building, according to your directions." With one exception, no order was specified and that particular item reads "Capitals 10 in[ches] diamt. (Tower of the winds)".[173] There is no existing documentation as to where these capitals were to be installed and the Annex was lost to a fire in 1895, but their reduced scale suggests they were meant to be tucked away on the interior. More to the point, their presence on this extension to Jefferson's quintessentially Roman Rotunda, even if on the Annex, directly recalls Latrobe's own subverting gesture, his successful efforts at placing the Attic in the Capitol, even if likewise it had been relegated there to minor vestibules.

Walter's use of the Attic was of a very different sort. Recalling Latrobe's use of national orders of his own invention at the Capitol, the corncob and magnolia, but especially the 1816 tobacco-leaf columns that he specifically linked to the Attic and which had been introduced into the new Senate vestibule, Walter followed this last example and created yet another tobacco-leaf capital modeled on the Attic for his new Senate wing (Figure 47). Pressured by the expansion of the Union—by 1850 there were thirty-one states—the Senate called for expanded congressional chambers, accommodation that was best achieved by architectural extensions to the original structure rather than by renovation. A competition for designs followed and Mills and Walter emerged as the frontrunners, but following a deadlock when the House and Senate could not agree on a winner, the choice devolved to President Millard Fillmore. In June 1851, at the suggestion of Daniel

---

[171] Quoted from "Memorial of Robert Mills, in relation to the enlargement of the Capitol," May 20, 1850; *Table of Reports of Committees; Printed by Order of the Senate of the United States, First Session, Thirty First Congress 1849–50*, no. 145, 8 (Washington DC: U.S.Government Printing Office).

[172] Mills, "Architecture in Virginia," 41.

[173] Helen M. Gallagher, *Robert Mills, Architect of the Washington Monument, 1781–1855* (New York: Columbia University Press, 1935), 46, in an error often repeated by subsequent writers, dates the letter to 1822. It is correctly noted, but without any further discussion by Liscombe. *Altogether American*, 340, n. 144. Mills's "Of the manner of executing a certain Building proposed to be added to the Rotunda on the north side of the University Buildings," January 3, 1851, speaks of cast-iron columns and pillars being installed, but without any specificity as to the orders. One of the cast-iron Corinthian capitals from the façade survives in ruinous condition and is preserved at the university.

Figure 47. Thomas Ustick Walter, Tobacco leaf capital.

Webster, his Secretary of State, Fillmore appointed Walter, whose proposal it was felt was more sympathetic to the work of Latrobe and his predecessors.[174]

Then at the height of his career and the nation's leading public architect, Walter was an avid proponent of the Greek Revival who frequently consulted

---

[174] For Walter at the Capitol, see Herman T. Rosenberger, "Thomas Ustick Walter and the Completion of the United States Capitol," *Records of the Columbia Historical Society* 50 (1952): 273–322; Allen, *History of the Capitol*, 187–335; Scott, *Temple of Liberty*, 95–100; and James M. Goode, "Thomas U. Walter and the Search for Propriety," in *Designing and Decorating a National Icon*, ed. Kennon, 85–109.

the *Antiquities of Athens* and as has been seen also occasionally looked to Lafever's plate 11. Now in creating a national order he would follow Latrobe's personal example, but there is evidence that the revived idea of using national capitals with vegetal motifs was not his own, but came from someone whose taste was almost diametrically opposed, the military engineer Montgomery C. Meigs. Following reports of fraud among some of Walter's underlings though not by the architect himself, in March 1853 overall responsibility for the project was shifted to Meigs. Initially Walter welcomed the change, as he was then free "to devote myself to my legitimate professional duties."[175] Eventually, though, tensions set in and the relationship deteriorated as Meigs sought and obtained an ever-greater role in the building's plan and decorative schemes. However, where Walter preferred simplicity and restraint, Meigs, no longer affected by the lingering fears of a revived wasteful imperial splendor that had deterred many of the founding fathers, sought to enrich the building with extensive colorful decorative schemes. Walter, by contrast, saw only stylistic corruption in such gaudy display and preferred instead republican chasteness.[176]

By the introduction of paintings, sculpture, and assorted minor arts, Meig's introduced an extensive American iconographic scheme into the Capitol, whether through the introduction of historical narratives or in his choice of ornament. It must have been this interest in national features that first drew him to Latrobe's naturalized capitals as a prototype suitable for the new construction. Writing in his diary for July 12, 1854, he describes the clay model of a capital then being developed in collaboration with the sculptor Francis Vincenzi, which closely followed the conventions of the Corinthian order, but with tobacco and maize leaves above and celery or acanthus below. Although he noted that the result "does not resemble any capital which I have ever seen," formally it clearly follows a Corinthian format.[177] When completed, the model was copied for the paired columns that lined the corridor leading to the new Senate chamber in the new south extension.

At the Capitol's opposite end, on the ground floor of the new House extension, there was a central corridor, the Hall of Columns (Figure 48), marked by a double colonnade fourteen columns long, which ran the length of the new wing.[178] If the

---

[175] Walter to Dr. R. Gardner, February 22, 1854, quoted from Goode, "Search for Propriety," 94. For more on Meigs and Walter, see Russell F. Weigley, *Quartermaster General of the Union Army, A Biography of M.C. Meigs* (New York: Columbia University Press, 1959), 65–98 passim; and David W. Miller, *Second Only to Grant, Quartermaster General Montgomery V. Meigs* (Shippensburg, PA: White Mane Books, 2000), 26–54.

[176] For Meigs and the Capitol decorations, see Barbara Wolanin, "Meigs the Art Patron," in *Montgomery V. Meigs and the Building of the Nation's Capitol*, eds. William C. Dickinson, Dean A. Herrin, and Donald R. Kennon (Athens, OH: United States Capitol Historical Society by Ohio University Press, 2001), 133–65.

[177] Meigs accompanied his entry with a small drawing of the capital: *Capitol Builder: The Shorthand Journals of Montgomery C. Meigs 1853–1859, 1861*, ed. Wendy Wolff, (Washington, DC: U.S. Government Printing Office, 2001), 86. Vincenti worked at the Capitol 1853–58.

[178] For the Hall, see Allen, *History of the Capitol*, 240–41; and Scott, *Temple of Liberty*, 135.

Figure 48. Thomas Ustick Walter, Hall of Columns, United States Capitol.

capitals outside the Senate were after an idea of Meigs, for those beneath the House, Walter adamantly claimed credit. Writing to Charles Fowler, a New York iron founder in February 1855, he noted: We shall have a new range of elegantly wrought marble columns of a new order to my own design, with delicately sculpted tobacco leaves, thistle, cotton, & c., costing a mint of money."[179] These, which carefully follow the example of Latrobe's Attic columns, retained the pronounced roundness of the order and the bottom row of acanthus leaves, while above quoting from his columns in the Senate vestibule, Walter substituted tobacco leaves for waterleaves and placed thistles rather than simple stems between. Whatever his original intention, no cotton plants were included.

---

[179] Walter to Charles Fowler, February 19, 1855, quoted from Allen, *History of the Capitol*, 241.

13

Yet the Attic Order Persists

— A Capital Problem —

By the time Attic capitals were installed in Charlottesville and the American variant in the Capitol, the Greek Revival style was well on its way to decline. Mills would die in 1855 and Walters, despite his prior prejudices, had by then begun working in the Italianate style, which with the Gothic Revival and French Empire would dominate American architecture in succeeding decades.[180] With regard to federal construction, buildings that were meant to represent national authority, the later governmental works of Ammi B. Young provide an excellent example of this stylistic shift and at the same time a peculiar and confirmatory lingering use of the Attic. Well before Young's aforementioned Boston Custom House was completed in 1847, a Gothic sympathizer writing in the 1844 *North American Review* already was attacking its parochial Grecianism. It was criticized as "a leaf cut out of Stuart's Athens, that inexhaustible quarry of bad taste."[181] After 1852, by which time Young had assumed the office of Supervising Architect of the Office of Construction of the Treasury Department, he too underwent a marked and meaningful change in taste. Abandoning the classicism that he had personally favored and which long prevailed for governmental edifices, his federal work assumed an Italianate appearance.[182] Nevertheless, despite these exteriors, several times he did retain Greek detailing and on the interiors of his custom houses in Galena, Illinois, 1857–59 (Figure 49), and Chicago, 1855–60, he continued to use Attic capitals.[183]

Needless to say the Civil War, 1861–65, brought about a hiatus to governmental building at all levels and would have put a damper on all other architectural design and construction. And during Reconstruction, with the resumption of construction in America's cities, it was the Second Empire style of Baron Hausmann's rebuilding of Paris in the 1850s under Napoleon III that came into the ascendancy, leaving little room if any at all for classical details like the Attic. But with the new century and following the example of the White City of the 1893 Chicago World's Fair, Classical architecture came back into favor. Perhaps, even if not wholly Greek, it was imagined yet again as a national style. And once more on both the smaller domestic and the monumental scale, including private and governmental commissions, the Attic order reappeared, persisting until well into the twentieth century, but much devoid of its previous particular pertinence for America. In scale an example

---

[180] Lafever, for example, turned to the Italianate and Gothic, in the late 1840s; see Landy, *Lafever*, 159–79.

[181] For this quote and further on the critical reception, see Wodehouse, "Architectural Projects," 77. Also see, Bluestone, "City and Aesthetic Reserve," 133–36.

[182] Young had also contended for the Capitol extensions in 1850, for which, see Wodehouse, "Architectural Projects," 83–84 n. 11.

[183] See Daniel M. Bluestone, "Ammi Burnham Young's 1850s Federal Customhouse Designs," *Winterthur Annual* 25 (1990): 146–49.

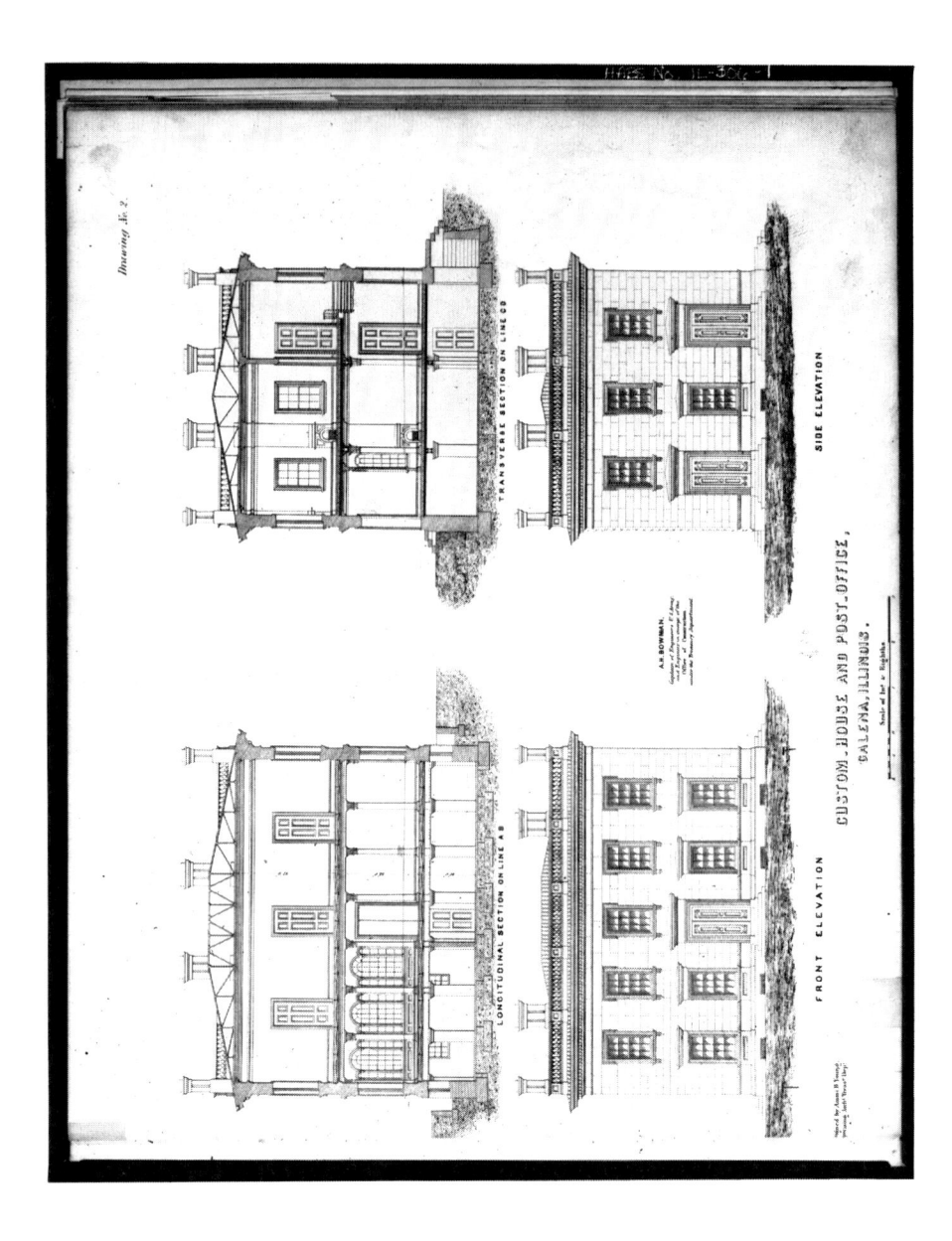

Figure 49. Ammi B. Young, *Custom-House and Post-Office, Sections and Elevations*, Galena, Illinois, 1857–59.

— A Capital Problem —

Figure 50. Egerton Swartwout, Mary Baker Eddy grave, Mt. Auburn Cemetery, Cambridge, Massachusetts, 1915.

of the former use is Egerton Swartwout's colonnade memorializing Mary Baker Eddy's (d. 1910) grave (Figure 50) beside Halcyon Lake, Mt. Auburn Cemetery, Cambridge, Massachusetts. For the latter there is the giant order of columns and pilasters on Cass Gilbert's Chase Brass and Copper headquarters (Figure 51) in Waterbury, Connecticut, 1917–19.[184] To cite just a few other uses that also demonstrate the giant order's continuing variety of applications, there are churches, the Second Baptist Church, 1922, Savannah, Georgia, whose transformation to the Greek was by Henrik Wallin, a local architect, and the First Baptist Church, Sarasota, Florida, by George Washington Kramer; houses, notably Henry Ford's Richmond Hill, Georgia, estate by another Savannah architect, Cletus Bergen; and yet again a federal building in New Bern, North Carolina, 1932–34, designed by Robert F. Smallwood, a native with an architectural practice in New York City.[185] The Attic also found applications

---

[184] Barbara S. Christen, "A 'New' New England: Proposals for New Haven and Waterbury, Connecticut," *Cass Gilbert, Life and Work: Architect of the Public Domain*, eds. Barbara S. Christen and Steven Flanders (New York: W.W. Norton, 2001), 188–90.

[185] For the Ford mansion, see F. Leslie Long and Lucy B. Long, *The Henry Ford Estate at Richmond Hill, Georgia* (Richmond Hill, GA: F.L. Long, 1998); and for New Bern, Peter B. Sandbeck, *The Historic Architecture of New Bern and Craven County, North Carolina* (New Bern, NC: Tryon Palace Commission, 1988), 154, 368–69.

Figure 51. Cass Gilbert, Chase Brass and Copper Company (now Chase Municipal Building), Waterbury, Connecticut, 1917–19.

— A Capital Problem —

at academic institutions, for example, at the University of North Carolina at Chapel Hill, on the entry portico to the Coats Building, 1938–39 by H. Raymond Weeks, and in the internal rotunda to Eggers and Higgins's Morehead Foundation, 1947–49. Also in North Carolina, after 1963 Leslie N. Boney would several times use the Attic order for the campus of what was to become the University of North Carolina at Wilmington. Strikingly, what the bulk of these locations further confirm is the South's lingering partiality for classical architecture, as does this final example, a Memphis, Tennessee, home designed c. 1940 by a local firm, Furbinger and Ehrman for Dr. T. Moore. Named for his wife, Grace, with the name retained as Graceland (Figure 52) this home was sold in the mid-1950s to Elvis Presley.[186] Thus, in a manner of speaking, the use of the Attic order is bracketed by two national pilgrimage sites, ironically, one, the earlier, the national Capitol, being the major republican monument to the nation's having deposed one king, whereas the other, the later, Graceland, has come to be seen as America's last royal residence, the home of an erstwhile king, albeit of the kingdom of rock and roll. Doubtless, however, few visitors to either location have any real recognition of this particular detail or its particular significance, its declarative and especially American presence. Yet again the Attic has become an architectural detail devoid of any national meaning and become instead an ornamental throwback to some ancient time.

---

[186] See Karal Ann Marling, *Graceland: Going Home with Elvis* (Cambridge, MA: 1996), 137, 143, 145, who erroneously identifies the capitals as Egyptian and thus reflective of Memphis, a city with Egyptian allusions.

Figure 52. Furbinger and Ehrman, Graceland, Memphis, Tennessee, c. 1940.

Index

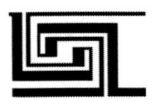

— Index —

A

Acanthus leaf design, 12, 14, 99, 125
The Adam Style in America, 28
Adam, James, 21, 22, 25, 26, 28, 35, 37, 74, 99
Adam, Robert, 21, 22, 23, 24, 25, 26, 28, 35, 37, 74, 99
Adams, John, 45
Adelphi, 25, 37
Aescalapius, Temple of, 21
The American Builder's Companion, 37
Amherst College, 18
Andronikos, horologium of, 9
Antiquities, 4, 8–14, 20, 28, 50–51, 55, 83, 92, 99
The Antiquities of Athens, 8–9, 20, 51, 55, 83, 99
Arch of Theseus, 51
Ashdown House, 29–31, 51
Asher, Benjamin, 37–38
Asia Minor, 9
Assumption of the Blessed Virgin Mary Basilica, 55–58, 65
Athenian Choragic Monument, 50

B

Baltimore diocese cathedral, 55–58, 65
Bank of Pennsylvania, 55
Barlow, Joel, 7
Basilica of the Assumption of the Blessed Virgin Mary, 55–58, 65
Basire, James, 4, 13
Beauties of Modern Architecture, 100–101
Bergen, Cletus, 133
Boney, Leslie N., 135
Boston Custom House, 131
Boyd, Sterling M., 28
Bragg, Aristabulus, 3
Breweries, 3
Brownell, Charles E., 10, 12, 18, 30, 36, 45–46, 48, 55, 58, 61, 65, 74, 79

Bulfinch, Charles, 35–37, 39, 70, 73–74, 76–80, 84, 87–88, 90, 92, 94–95

C

Cambridge, Massachusetts, 133
Canonical orders, 12, 37, 45
Capitol, 43–52
Carroll, John, 55
Carvers of stone, 37, 48
Cass Gilbert's Chase Brass and Copper headquarters, 133–134
Cast capitals, 29
Cathedral for diocese of Baltimore, 55–58, 65
Chambers, William, 8, 17, 21, 50, 65, 68, 74, 121
Chapel Hill, 135
Chase Brass and Copper Company. *See* Chase Municipal Building
Chase Municipal Building, 134
Chestnut Street Theatre, Philadelphia, 75
Chicago World's Fair, 131
Chimney pieces, 66, 69
Choragic Monument, 12, 50, 94
Civil Architecture, 8, 50
Civil War, 115, 131
Clark, John, 9
Coade catalog, 30, 35
Coade's Artistic Stone Manufactory, 29
Cohen, Jeffrey A., 10, 18, 30, 35–36, 41, 45–46, 48, 55, 58, 61, 65, 74
Colonnades, 46, 61, 65, 76, 84, 92, 94, 122, 125, 133
"Composed Doric," 21–22
Composite order, 21
Congress, Library of, 36, 40, 47, 49, 67, 74, 77–78, 88–89, 132
Cooper, James Fenimore, 3, 18
Corinthian style, 8, 12, 14, 20–21, 35, 37, 45–46, 48, 50–51, 55, 58, 65–

Index

66, 74, 94, 99, 104, 107, 121–123, 125
Corncob order, 66
Corruption, stylistic, 28, 125
Croghan, William, 115
Custom House, 105
Cyrrhestes, Andronicus, 9, 12

D

Dakin, James, 18–19, 92, 95, 99, 102–103, 109
Dalton, Richard, 9–10
Davis, Alexander Jackson, 7, 76, 78–79, 83, 89–90, 92–95, 99, 110
Dickinson College, 55
Diocletian, 21, 23–24
Dorians, 12
Doric style, 8, 12, 20–22, 25, 35, 45–48, 50–51, 65, 84, 88–89, 92–94, 104, 110, 121

E

Eclecticism, 28
Eddy, Mary Baker, 133
Effingham, Eva, 3
Egyptian influences, 9, 58, 76
Elliot, William P., 90

F

Female Academy, Lexington, Mississippi, 84
Fillmore, Millard, 123–124
Fireplaces, 68, 70, 83, 87
Ford, Henry, 83, 131
Fowler, Charles, 125
Franklin, Benjamin, 35
Franzoni, Giuseppe, 48, 68
Frieze, 46, 48, 50

G

Gallier, James, 95, 99, 102–103, 106
Gilbert, Cass, 133–134

Gilmer, Stephen H., 76
Giovanni, Andrei, 48
Godefroy, Maximillian, 58, 61
Gothic Revival, 131
Government Street Presbyterian Church, LA, 99, 103, 110
Graceland, 135–136
Grecian School, 3
Greek Revival, 3, 8–10, 12, 17–18, 25, 35–37, 41, 58, 66, 73, 79–80, 84, 89, 93, 95, 104–106, 109–110, 115, 121, 124, 131
Greenwich Hospital, 20–21

H

Hall of Columns, 125–126
Hallett, Stephen, 45
Hamilton, William, 27–28
Hammond, David, 89
Harper, Robert Goodloe, 58
Harvard, 35
Hatfield, George, 45
Hausmann, Baron, 131
Hermitage, 89–92, 115
The Hermitage, 89–92
Hewitt, Gordon, 115
Home as Found, 3
Horologium of Andronikos, 9
House of Representatives, 45, 50, 52, 65
Hoxey house, 115
Hume, William, 89–90
Hybridized style, 7
Hydrants, public, 86–88

I

Ionians, 12
Ionic style, 8, 12, 20–21, 29, 35, 45, 48, 51, 55, 65–66, 76, 83–84, 95, 104, 121
Italianate style, 131

Index

J
Jay, John, 115–116
Jefferson, Thomas, 7, 12, 35, 45–46, 48, 50–51, 65–68, 121–123

K
Kalorama, 7
Kelly, Alison, 29, 36–37
Kennedy, Roger G., 35
Kerrison house, 115
Knox, William, 115
Kramer, George Washington, 133

L
Lansdowne House, 25
"Lantern of Demosthenes," 12, 50
Latin orders, 7, 45
Latrobe, Benjamin Henry, 3, 7, 9–10, 12, 18, 28–31, 35–36, 39–41, 45–52, 55–61, 63, 65–71, 73–74, 76, 79, 83–84, 86–88, 92, 94–95, 104, 121–125, 127
Le Roy, Julien-David, 9
Lefever, Minard, 95, 99–102
Lenthall, John, 7, 50, 52
Library Company, 35
Library of Congress, 36, 40, 47, 49, 67, 74, 77, 88–89, 132
London Society of Dilettanti, 7
Louisiana Hose Company, 18
Ludlum, Richard, 115

M
Madison, James, 65, 69
Magnin, Joseph, 39
Massachusetts State House, 37, 39, 74, 95
McComb, John M., 39, 104
Meigs, Montgomery C., 125, 127
Metopes, 46
Mill Hill, 36–37

Mississippi State Capitol, 85–86
"Modern Composite Capital," 25
Monticello, 68, 120
Mrs. Coade's Stone, 29

N
Napoleon, 58, 129
New Orleans, 18–19, 73, 84, 95, 99, 102, 109
New York City Hall, 41
New York University, 92
Newton, William, 9–10, 20–21, 76, 88
Nichols, William, 83–86, 93–95
Nicholson, Peter, 35
Norris, John, 105–106

O
Ottoman Turks, 7
Oxford, Radcliffe Observatory, 17, 92

P
Pain, William, 25, 27–28, 35
Palladians, 51
Palladio, 7, 35, 50
Pantheon, 120
Porches, 9–10, 12, 17, 20, 25, 29, 36, 90, 92
The Practical Builder, 25, 27
Presley, Elvis, 133
Public hydrants, 86, 88

R
Radcliffe Observatory, Oxford, 17, 92
Raleigh, N.C. State House, 95
Reconstruction, 10, 45, 92–93, 131
Reiff, Joseph, 89–90, 104
Renaissance, 7, 14
Republicanism, 45, 80
Revett, Nicholas, 7–10, 12–14, 20–21, 35, 50–51, 104, 110
Reynolds, Sir Joshua, 28

Index

Riou, Stephen, 12, 35, 46
Roman Forum, 50
Roman Pantheon, 120
Royal Academy, 12, 28

S
Second Empire style, 131
Senate, 45–46, 48, 65–66, 68, 70, 74, 79–80, 84, 95, 123, 125, 127
Shugborough House, 17
Sicily, 9
Smallwood, Robert F., 133
Soane, John, 12, 17–18, 25
South Carolina College, 88
Stone carvers, 37, 48
Strickland, William, 73–75, 83, 121
Stylistic corruption, 28, 125
Supreme Court, 65, 79, 84–86
Swartwout, Egerton, 133

T
Temple of Aescalapius, 21
Temple of the Winds, 48, 65, 74, 84. *See also* Tower of the Winds
Thornton, William, 45, 50, 122
Three Sisters, New Orleans, 102
Tobacco leaf design, 66, 68, 123–125, 127
Tower of the Winds, 3, 10–12, 17–18, 20, 55, 90, 92, 123
Traquair's Philadelphia marble yard, 68
Triton wind vane, 10
Turks, 7, 80
Tuscaloosa, 83–84, 99, 106

U
United States Capitol, 43–52
United States Custom House, 105
University of North Carolina at Chapel Hill, 135
University of North Carolina at Wilmington, 135
University of Virginia, 121–122
Ustick, Thomas, 73, 121, 124, 126

V
Vincenzi, Francis, 125
Vitruvius translation, 9–10, 12, 20

W
Walk, Exchange, 61
Walker, Anthony, 11
Wallin, Henrik, 133
War of 1812, 45, 69
Ware, Isaac, 7, 12, 50
Warren, Russell, 115
Waterleaf design, 21, 83, 90, 95, 99, 127
Watkin, David, 8, 17–18, 20–21, 35
Webster, Daniel, 79, 124
Weeks, H. Raymond, 135
White City, Chicago World's Fair, 131
Woodlands, Philadelphia mansion, 25, 27–28
World's Fair, 131
Wyatt, James, 17–18, 92

Y
Yazoo City, 84